Cognitive Science Series, 1

Semantic and Conceptual Development

An Ontological Perspective

Frank C. Keil

Harvard University Press
Cambridge, Massachusetts
and London, England
1979

Library of Congress Cataloging in Publication Data

Keil, Frank C 1952–
 Semantic and conceptual development.

 (Cognitive science series; 1)
 Includes bibliographical references and index.
 1. Cognition in children. 2. Knowledge, Theory of.
3. Psycholinguistics. 4. Semantics. I. Title.
II. Series.
BF723.C5K4   155.4'13   79-10491
ISBN 0-674-80100-8

Designed by Mike Fender

235175

To Kristi

Preface

Several years ago I read a paper entitled "Types and Ontology" by the philosopher Fred Sommers, in which he argued that ontological knowledge obeyed certain structural constraints. It seemed to me that these constraints might be viewed as cognitive in nature. In addition, ontological knowledge appeared to be a basic form of knowledge that was intimately related to a wide variety of semantic and conceptual phenomena. At about the same time I became convinced by the work of Noam Chomsky and Dan Osherson, among others, that the acquisition of knowledge in virtually any conceptual domain was guided and facilitated by a set of a priori constraints, many of which were specifically tailored for that domain. I became intrigued with the idea of studying how ontological knowledge develops within the guidelines set down by certain constraints, on the chance that this avenue of research might lead to new insights into semantic and conceptual development.

I decided to explore the psychological implications of Sommers' theory by attempting to translate his theory into psychological constructs and by devising empirical tests for those constructs. The project involved a series of studies with adults and children. Although research of this sort on ontological knowledge and its development is still in an early stage, suggestive findings have emerged, which seem to shed new light on aspects of semantic and conceptual development. Beyond the specific findings, however, the research also suggests a general strategy for studying cognitive development. Instead of trying to pinpoint those aspects of conceptual structure that change with development, the focus is on determining those aspects that remain invariant. What are the constraints on natural conceptual structures, and what is their role in the acquisition of those structures? One of the most vexing questions in cognitive psychology concerns how children learn such an extraordinary amount with such ease and rapidity. The answer may lie in the discovery of formal constraints. If, for example, within the infinitely large class of logically possible conceptual structures, children (and adults) were limited by constraints to a much smaller set, then the learning task would appear less of a mystery.

Many people have contributed along the way to this book. Unfortunately it is not possible to list them all, but I must mention those who have especially influenced the outcome. Without question, a primary obligation is to Dan Osherson, who as adviser, colleague, and friend had an impact on virtually every part of the book. Without the training and instruction that I received from him it is unlikely that I ever would have been able to execute the program of research. My debt to him is not easily repaid.

Special thanks must go to: Rochel Gelman, who made cogent remarks on different versions of the manuscript and helped to sharpen my understanding of that species called "children"; Lila Gleitman, whose advice and confidence were invaluable and whose intuitions about language were unsurpassed; Susan Carey, who carefully read several versions of the manuscript and provided a wealth of helpful comments and criticisms; Rich Warner, who helped me to understand more fully the philosophical implications of this work; and Jan Krueger, who offered an incisive commentary at all levels from the theoretical to the stylistic.

Colleagues at Cornell who read various sections of the book at different stages of development and had frequent discussions with me concerning it include Lynn Cooper, Jim Cunningham, Bob Dworkin, Jim Farber, E. J. Gibson, and Dick Neisser. I especially wish to thank J. J. Gibson for an extremely careful reading of the entire manuscript and for copious comments on virtually every page.

The studies reported here would not have been possible without the help of several other individuals. John Carroll and Bruce Rideout, as research associates, collected much of the data. In addition, both of them read the entire manuscript and made useful suggestions. I am deeply appreciative of their exhaustive and dedicated work. Pam Fasick and Ali Toruella, who were helpful in the preschool and Puerto Rican studies, respectively, showed great sophistication and dedication in collecting data. Thanks are also owed to Kevin Cotter for generously providing the proof appearing in Appendix B.

I am deeply indebted to the staffs and students at several Ithaca area elementary schools and preschools. Without their cheerful cooperation, it would not have been possible to conduct much of the research.

Ann Kleinsasser did a masterful job of typing the manuscript under relentless time pressure, often managing to read my writing even when I could not. Thanks also to Edie Clark, for help with the typing and for taking care of the financial details of the research, and to Jane Jorgenson, for executing the artwork under unreasonably harsh time constraints.

Several individuals at Harvard University Press have been very helpful in all stages of production of this book. I especially thank Eric Wanner, who has been an ideal editor.

I am grateful to the National Science Foundation (grant #BNS 78-06200) for supporting much of the research reported in this book.

Finally, I owe the largest debt to my wife Kristi. She has cheerfully made sacrifice after sacrifice so that I might finish the book. She has discussed with me and critically evaluated virtually every concept in it, often at times when she would much rather be asleep. She has constantly provided support and encouragement when it was needed most. I hope that sometime in the near future I may be able to reciprocate. I should also apologize here to two loyal if less scholarly friends, Amber and Bonnie, who without quite understanding why patiently waited for many late meals and never complained about frequently missing walks along the railroad tracks and swims in the lake.

Contents

xi

Figures

Tables

Semantic and Conceptual Development

1 | Introduction

WHAT CONSTRAINTS ARE THERE on human knowledge, and how do these constraints guide the acquisition of knowledge? This question is basic to the study of human cognition. My purpose is to ask the question within a restricted cognitive domain known as ontological knowledge and to explore how the development of ontological knowledge influences conceptual and semantic development.

Ontological knowledge refers to one's conception of the basic categories of existence, of what sorts of things there are. Such a definition may sound vague and metaphysical. Direct psychological data for this type of knowledge are hard to come by. Intuitions about the structure of such knowledge are not easily accessible. It would seem no more fruitful to ask subjects what the basic categories of existence are than to ask them what the structure of language is. This lack of direct psychological evidence might suggest that ontological knowledge does not exist as a separate cognitive domain. Such a suggestion, however, would be incorrect.

Just as language structure can be discovered by examining intuitions about grammaticality, ontological structure can be uncovered by looking at intuitions about other phenomena. Ontological knowledge has unique properties and is highly structured. Moreover, it constrains the nature of semantic and conceptual knowledge. This constraining role is the basic reason for choosing ontological knowledge as an area of study. An understanding of how such knowledge develops should lead to insights into semantic and conceptual development. Prior to any developmental studies, however, it is necessary to develop a precise and empirically based theory of the structure of ontological knowledge in adults.

1

It is often customary to begin construction of a new theory with a critique of other approaches to the problem. Such an approach is not feasible in this case because of the paucity of psychological research on ontological knowledge. For this reason the psychological phenomena that the theory is meant to account for must be considered first. With these observable phenomena as reference points, it is possible to define their theoretical relation to ontological knowledge. Once this relation is understood, its relevance to other psychological research can be explored. While rarely discussed explicitly, ontological knowledge is often tacitly presupposed in current psychological research. Moreover, it strongly influences the nature of those theories and explains a wide variety of seemingly unrelated phenomena. Because the psychological literature is so sparse on the subject, the main insight into theory construction in this area must come from the philosophical and linguistic literature.

A coherent and empirically based account of ontological knowledge and its psychological consequences makes possible the study of the development of that knowledge. Once the precise links are established between observable phenomena and underlying ontological knowledge, those phenomena can be used to construct representations of a child's ontological knowledge throughout development. My goal is therefore to develop a formal model specifying the nature of ontological knowledge and its relation to more overt psychological phenomena, and to use this model to explore the development of ontological knowledge and its influence on semantic and conceptual development.

2 | The Phenomena

THERE ARE four psychological phenomena, among others, that are surface manifestations of underlying ontological knowledge. They are anomalous sentences, natural classes, similar classes, and natural copredications.

Sentences That Do Not Make Sense

The first phenomenon is that some sentences are neither true nor false; they are anomalous. Consider the following examples:

1. The cow was brown.
2. The recess was an hour long.
3. The table was made of wood.
4. The cow was green.
5. The recess was one microsecond long.
6. The table was made of linguini.
7. The cow was an hour long.
8. The recess was thin.
9. The table was hungry.

Sentences 1–3 would normally be considered true, while 4–6 would normally be considered false. Sentences 7–9, however, are anomalous. Neither they nor their negations make any sense, assuming that the negation applies to the predicate and is not a denial of the whole sentence. Although 4–6 are likely to be false, they do make sense in that one knows what it means for a cow to be green even though the actuality may be highly unlikely. By contrast, one does not know what it means for a table to be hungry. To put it differently, sentences 7–9 fail to make sense because one cannot imagine any set of circumstances under which they could be true. How, for example, could one possibly tell if a recess were thin?

Some or all of sentences 7–9 could be made acceptable through an elaborate use of metaphor or ellipsis. For example, a recess might be sensibly considered thin if "thin" is metaphorically taken to mean "short in duration." Or a cow might be considered an hour long if, by ellipsis, what is really meant is that it took the cow an hour to do something. These and other instances of metaphor and ellipsis can be reasonably distinguished from literal usage.

Naturalness of Classes

The second phenomenon is that humans find some classes more natural than others. For example, class A consists entirely of the subclasses humans, liquids, and numbers, while class B consists entirely of the subclasses humans, plants, and animals. The phenomenon is that class B is more natural than class A. Class A does not seem to "hang together" to form any sort of coherent, natural whole, while class B can be seen as forming a coherent class of living things. Or compare class C, consisting solely of machines, events, and sentences, and class D, consisting solely of liquids, gases, and aggregates. Class D is more natural as it forms a coherent whole of physical things that have no shape. This phenomenon does not encompass all senses of naturalness that could apply to classes. For example, it does not include the sense in which the class of all robins is more natural than the class of animals that have three feet.

Similarity of Natural Classes

The third phenomenon is that humans may find a given class of objects more similar to some classes than to others. As in the case of naturalness of classes, there are many ways in which two classes can be similar or dissimilar. This phenomenon only involves the particular dimension of similarity shown in the following examples: humans are more similar to other animals than they are to plants, humans are more similar to plants than they are to liquids, and plants are more similar to liquids than they are to events. It does not involve, for example, the sense in which chickens are more similar to turkeys than they are to falcons.

Naturalness of Copredications

The fourth phenomenon is that only certain pairs of predicates can be combined sensibly or naturally. "Combined" in this sense means using any of the classical two-place logical connectives: "and," "or," and "if . . . . then." Consider the following examples:

10. X is tall and x is red.
11. If x is honest, then x is heavy.
12. If x is ungrammatical, then x is about Socrates.
13. Either x is fat or x is hungry.
14. X is tall and x is about Socrates.
15. If x is honest, then x is an hour long.
16. If x is ungrammatical, then x is waterproof.
17. Either x is fat or x is false.

Sentences 10–13 are allowable copredications in that they are conceivable. Sentences 14–17 are so bizarre that it is impossible even to conceive of them or to imagine any x that could satisfy them.

Two caveats are necessary. First, not all copredications that are inconceivable are included within this phenomenon. In particular, direct contradictions of the form "if x is round, then x is square" are not considered the same phenomenon. Support for this distinction comes from the fact that the negation of either predicate in a contradiction yields an allowable copredication, while the negation of "honest" in sentence 15 is still inconceivable, that is, "If x is dishonest, then x is an hour long."

A second class of nonnatural copredications is also not included in the fourth phenomenon. An example of such a copredication would be "X is sincere and x likes to eat lukewarm enchiladas while riding on a skateboard." Such a copredication seems nonnatural in a different sense. It is not always easy to distinguish between the two kinds of naturalness. One distinction may be that, in the second case, it is quite possible to think of something that satisfies both predicates, no matter how unlikely that something is. In contrast to this property of likelihood, the fourth phenomenon involves cases where it is not even possible to conceive of something that satisfies both predicates.

The fourth phenomenon can be stated in two other ways that have different connotations. If concepts are defined as logical combinations of various predicates, then this phenomenon can be seen as describing a necessary condition for natural concepts. Natural concepts are those that use predicates all of which are copredicable with one another. This is not a sufficient condition in that a sincere, enchilada-eating skateboard rider is not what one might ordinarily consider a natural concept even though it is allowed by this phenomenon. It might be more appropriate to say that this phenomenon distinguishes conceivable from inconceivable concepts. This is closer to the truth but still is not completely correct since some inconceivable concepts may be inconceivable merely because of their complexity. Inconceivable concepts of this type are analogous to sentences with multiple center-embedded clauses which are grammatical but cannot be processed by the normal listener.

The second restatement of the fourth phenomenon is in terms of possible empirical laws. In attempts to describe and explain the world, people often propose laws in the form: $(\forall x)(Px \rightarrow Qx)$. The phenomenon distinguishes between possible laws of this form and impossible ones. Possible laws are those that a human would propose. A law is possible if and only if P and Q are copredicable and if and only if both P and Q can be sensibly applied to the instantiation for x.

A theory is needed to account for these four phenomena in a unified fashion. The theory need not be restricted to these four phenomena, however. Other phenomena that it could encompass include metaphor construction, certain forms of entailment, and possible lexical items.

The brief descriptions of the phenomena so far can also convey only an informal understanding of them. The precise boundaries of each of the phenomena will be brought into clearer focus by the formal theory and by empirical evidence.

3 | Developing a Theory

TO BE SUCCESSFUL, a theory must specify the nature of the knowledge that underlies and is responsible for the four phenomena. Fortunately, there is work in the philosophical literature that provides many of the components of a successful theory by drawing links between ontological categories and a phenomenon known as "predicability." Predicability is simply the phenomenon that only certain predicates can be combined with certain terms in a natural language. In fact, it is closely related to anomaly. Once the relation is shown between knowledge of ontological categories and predicability, the relations of that knowledge to the phenomena of similarity, naturalness of classes, and copredication are not difficult to discover. But before a theory of conceptual knowledge is developed, it is necessary to consider in detail what the goals of such a theory should be.

Goals

Chomsky (1965, 1975) argues that an ideal theory for any well-defined cognitive domain should satisfy certain conditions of adequacy. In discussing a theory of grammar, Chomsky distinguishes between three types of adequacy: observational, descriptive, and explanatory. A descriptively adequate theory is superior to an observationally adequate one, and an explanatorily adequate one is superior to a descriptively adequate one. One of the main goals of a theory of the four phenomena is to satisfy these levels of adequacy, especially the explanatory level. It is thus essential to understand precisely what satisfaction consists of at each level.

At the observational level, a syntactic theory is adequate if it is able to enumerate exhaustively all and only those sentences that are well formed, or grammatical, in a given language. Similarly, a theory of the four phenomena is observationally adequate to the extent that it is able to enumerate what sentences are anomalous, what classes are natural, what orderings of relative similarity occur between sets of classes, and what copredications are semantically acceptable.

A variety of theories can satisfy observational adequacy. For example, a phrase-structure grammar could provide an observationally adequate theory of syntax, as could a transformational generative grammar. But some observationally adequate theories seem to be clearly preferable over others, and the criterion of descriptive adequacy makes it possible to choose between sets of observationally adequate theories. A theory of syntax is descriptively adequate if it is able not only to enumerate all well-formed sentences but also to account for the constituent structures of sentences; that is, it must be able to reflect the speakers' intuitions about the underlying structures of sentences. Thus, a grammar of syntax should be able to generate different structures for ambiguous sentences. In an analogous fashion, a theory of the four phenomena, if descriptively adequate, should be able to capture higher level generalizations about the four phenomena. For example, a descriptively adequate theory might show that intuitions about anomaly are organized in a highly structured manner. In addition, it might explain all four phenomena with one unified account rather than with four virtually separate but nevertheless observationally adequate accounts.

Finally, at the explanatory level, a syntactic theory is adequate if it provides a set of general properties and constraints such that all and only the natural languages are formalizable under those constraints. That is, a theory of syntax is explanatorily adequate if it can determine for any novel language whether it is humanly natural. In many conceptual domains the naturalness-nonnaturalness distinction is not necessarily a dichotomy but can also be treated as a continuum. Osherson (1976), for example, discusses how simplicity metrics can be used to describe such continuums in various conceptual domains.

An important consequence of explanatory adequacy is stated by Chomsky (1965): "A theory of linguistic structure that aims for explanatory adequacy incorporates an account of linguistic universals, and it attributes tacit knowledge of these universals to the child. It proposes, then, that the child approaches the data with the presumption that they are drawn from a language of a certain antecedently well-defined type, his problem being to determine which of the (humanly) possible languages is that of the community in which he is placed. Language learning would be impossible unless this were the case" (p. 27). This means that an explanatorily adequate account for any conceptual domain should provide insights into how knowledge in that domain is acquired by positing constraints on what sorts of knowledge representations are conceptually natural.

A theory of the four phenomena will be explanatorily adequate to the extent that it is able to provide constraints on knowledge in the relevant conceptual domain such that those contraints result in the four intuitive phenomena. That is, if there is one knowledge structure that underlies the four phenomena, an explanatorily adequate theory must be able to specify the class of representations that are conceptually natural and to state what constraints are responsible for such a class. Moreover, a consequence of such a theory should be that it yields important insights into how that knowledge is acquired.

The criterion of explanatory adequacy cannot be satisfied completely. Rather, that criterion should be seen as a guiding tenet since, even if the constraints developed are incomplete or only partially correct, they will nontheless be a step toward achieving that goal. One issue that leads to modest expectations is the fact that the conceptual domain is not yet well defined. It is not possible to be sure that a theory is explanatorily adequate until one knows precisely the boundaries of the conceptual domain on which it focuses. Thus, if the domain were narrower than at first thought, further constraints might be necessary. In the case of a theory of the four phenomena, the conceptual domain is a body of knowledge hypothesized to be the basis for various intuitions. As the theory about that knowledge develops, there can be no certainty that one's understanding of the boundaries of that knowledge will not change. One might argue that the domain of inquiry includes all natural concepts, in which case one could hope to achieve only a small degree of explanatory adequacy. However, if the relevant conceptual domain is more restricted, it should be possible to provide a more complete account.

The satisfaction of explanatory adequacy in many domains can be seen as a "bootstrap" sort of operation by which, as one develops further constraints, one develops a better understanding of the boundaries of the conceptual domain for which the final constraints must be developed. Thus, for example, in the case of natural languages, the discovery of universal constraints on syntax bears crucially on the issue of the task specificity of language (Osherson and Wasow, 1976). The reason is that many of the more convincing arguments for elements of a language being task specific come from looking at linguistic universals which do not appear to have any nonlinguistic analogues. However, if it were to turn out that the knowledge structures responsible for syntax were nontask-specific, general cognitive structures, then the conceptual domain under investigation would have to be correspondingly expanded. These cautions should not be taken as predicting the failure of Chomsky's approach when applied to conceptual domains other than language. On the contrary, work by Osherson (1977) on natural logical connectives has successfully exploited Chomsky's approach by looking for general constraints that describe which connectives can be formalized by natural logics.

Once the goals are set forth a theory of the four phenomena can begin to be developed. The first step is to reflect on the nature of the knowledge that might underlie the four phenomena. It turns out to be a structured body of knowledge that is receptive to formal analysis.

Underlying Knowledge

The four phenomena seem to be closely related to one common kind of knowledge, namely knowledge of what predicates can be combined with what terms in a natural language, or "predicability." In turn, predicability itself is a reflection of an even more basic kind of human knowledge. This is the ontological knowledge that is the basis of a person's understanding of what sorts of things there are in the world and how they relate to each other.

Knowledge of predicability is organized in a highly structured manner. While it is theoretically possible for such knowledge to consist of an enormous list of all possible predicate-term pairs, human knowledge of predicability is not merely a list of this type. Instead, lists of predicates and lists of terms seem to interact according to various patterns that result in a much more economical representation than a simple list. For example, if one predicate can be sensibly combined with a term, it is also true that several other predicates can sensibly be combined with that term as well. If x is "honest," then x can also be "sincere," "asleep," "dead," "tall," and "heavy," but not "ungrammatical" or "an hour long." A more complicated pattern emerges when x is "tall." In that case, x can also be "red" or "heavy" and possibly, "honest," but never "an hour long." To put the concept in another way that illustrates certain superset-subset relations between classes of terms and predicates, all things that are honest can be tall but all things that are tall cannot necessarily be honest.

These examples illustrate two points about predicability: It determines which classes of predicates can be sensibly combined with which classes of terms, and it appears to involve hierarchical organization in that a predicate P_1 may be sensibly combined with a superset of the set of terms that can be sensibly combined with a predicate P_2. These informal conclusions do not in themselves explain the four phenomena, nor do they explain the link to ontological knowledge. Nevertheless, they are the basis for a long tradition of theorizing about ontological categories and their manifestation in natural language. Such notions about predicability have developed historically in the context of questions about the basic categories of existence.

A concept that is central to considerations of predicability is spanning. Various related definitions of spanning have been put forth by Sommers (e.g. 1963) and his associates (cf. Sayward, 1976). A simple and accurate summary would be: a predicate spans a term if and only if that predicate-term combination makes sense and can be assigned a truth value, which can be either true or false. Under this definition, the predicate "is green" spans "the frog" (probably truly) and "the milk" (probably falsely), but not "the idea."

Historical Antecedents

One of the best characterizations of predicability and its relation to categories appears in Aristotle's *Categories*. Although it would be an exaggeration to state that Aristotle had a clear conception of the special status of ontological categories vis-à-vis predicability in contrast to other taxonomic categories not demarcated by predicability, certain passages of his work nevertheless reveal that Aristotle was aware of the ways in which the phenomenon of predicability points toward ontological categories. Consider the following: "The differentiae of genera which are different and not subordinate to the other are themselves different in kind. For example animal and knowledge: footed, winged, aquatic, two-footed, are differentiae of animal, but none of these is a differentia of knowledge, one sort of knowledge does not differ from another by being two-footed.

However there is nothing to prevent genera subordinate one to the other from having the same differentiae. For the higher are predicated by the genera below them, so that all differentiae of the predicated genus will be differentiae of the subject also."

Aristotle here illustrates several important points. First, the concept of differentiae embodies the notion of a predicate being sensibly rather than truthfully applied to a term, as in spanning. For example, "two-footed" can be sensibly applied to all animals, but can be truthfully applied to only a small subset of animals.

The passage also illustrates how predicate classes and term classes seem to be arranged in some sort of hierarchical manner. Thus if two terms denote things of completely different types, such as "knowledge" and "animals," probably few if any differentiae will span both. But if term x denotes a class, such as "humans," that is subordinate to a class denoted by term y, such as "animals," then all differentiae that span term y can also span term x, although not necessarily vice versa.

Finally, the passage from *Categories* illustrates how the phenomenon is closely related to ontological knowledge. Aristotle's focus is not so much on the predicates, or "differentiae," and terms as on the objects that they denote. The superordinate-subordinate relations pertain primarily to the object classes themselves and only secondarily to classes of predicates and terms.

In a separate work, the *Topics*, where Aristotle elaborates on the notion of differentiae, he brings up another important point about predicability that figures crucially in modern theories. Aristotle notes that if a differentia appears to apply to objects in different genera, then the differentiae must be ambiguous. Thus, in English, "rational" is ambiguous when it applies to the different categories of "men" and "numbers."

Aristotle later modifies this claim when he points out that if a differentia spans a genus to which two genera of different kinds are subordinate, then the differentia will also span the two genera. Thus, under certain well-specified conditions, two terms from different categories could share a common predicate. This collection of observations can be unified in a coherent manner in a single theory. Moreover, since Aristotle's conjectures were not in English, they argue that predicability phenomena exist across languages.

Much more recently, Bertrand Russell (1924) and Gilbert Ryle (1938) have proposed theories that relate predicability to ontological categories. Sommers (1963) has reviewed their two approaches and synthesized a new theory out of a composite of the two.

Russell proposes that classes of things or types can be distinguished on the basis of the predicates that span them. Thus, two things are of the same type if they are both spanned by the same predicate. This simple formulation, however, leads to certain indeterminate situations. For example, "man" and "flea" would seem to be of the same type since they are both spanned by "is alive"; yet they are also of different types since only "man" is spanned by "is honest." An even worse consequence is that certain predicates, such as "is thought about," span all things and thereby obliterate all type distinctions. Black (1944) is one of the first of many to point out such problems with Russell's theory of types.

Ryle's theory is concerned with classes of predicates rather than classes of things. He claims that certain classes of predicates can be isolated on the basis of whether they apply to the same term or not. Thus, "is asleep" and "is hungry" are predicates of the same type since they both span terms that denote animals. In this context Ryle introduces the term "category mistake" to refer to those cases where two predicates from different categories are conjoined to create an anomaly, which is the same phenomenon as copredication. Category mistakes are also taken to refer to predicate-term anomalies.

Sommers illustrates how the criticisms of Russell's work can be applied to Ryle's account, in which certain indeterminacies about predicate classification are inherent. Thus, if two predicates are of the same type because they span the same term, then "is thought about" and "is hungry" should be of the same type since they both span "the dog." But they also are of different types since only "is thought about" spans "the chair." As in the case of Russell's theory, depending on what terms are chosen, two predicates might or might not be classified as being of the same type.

Other philosophers in looking at predicability and its relation to types have made closely related observations, even though none of their theories about predicability has been completely successful. Sommers' theory represents the most successful attempt to draw a link between predicability and ontology.

Sommers' Theory

Sommers (1959, 1963, 1965, 1971) has developed a theory that captures the essence of both Russell's and Ryle's observations yet avoids the problems that those theories encounter. He does so by imposing stricter criteria for the isolation of types. In Sommers' theory, there is a more structured relation between predicates and terms. Two terms are of the same type if and only if all predicates that span term t_1 also span t_2. Similarly, two predicates P_1 and P_2 are of the same type if they span exactly the same sets of terms. If term t_1 is spanned by a subset of the predicates that span t_2, then t_1 is a member of category C while t_2 is a member of a category subordinate to C. An essential part of this theory is that terms and predicates always sort themselves out in the same manner; that is, either two terms share exactly the same predicates, or one shares a subset of the other's predicates, or they share no predicates at all. There can never be a case where two terms have intersecting sets of predicates. If this were not so, there would be objects of indeterminate type.

Sommers' theory can best be illustrated in terms of a hierarchical tree structure (Fig. 1). Here and elsewhere throughout the text, predicates are shown in upper-case letters and terms in lower-case letters; solid lines represent predicate-predicate connections and dotted lines represent predicate-term connections.

Although the tree illustrated here follows the general principles of Sommers' theory, several changes and modifications have been made. First, the tree has many more nodes than the tree fragments presented by Sommers. Most of Sommers' trees include some subset of the same four terminal nodes, while this tree has nine terminal nodes. For this reason, any theoretical problems with the tree here should not be seen as necessarily problems with Sommers' original formulation.

There are also some notational changes. In Sommers' original discussion of tree structure, nodes were marked with absolute value signs ($|P|$) that represented not only the class of predicates but also all the terms spanned by that class of predicates. In the tree shown here, term classes are explicitly represented so that the various relations inherent in a tree structure can be seen more clearly.

The general rule to use in interpreting a tree structure is that a predicate spans all those terms that every predicate below it spans. For example, the predicate "is sick" spans all terms spanned by "is asleep" and "is wilted," namely all living things. The highest node in the tree contains predicates that span all terms, which seems intuitively correct since anything, physical or nonphysical, is interesting or not.

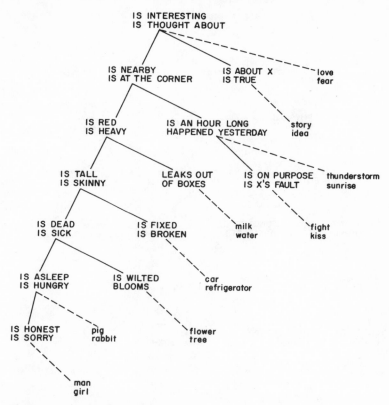

Figure 1. *Predicability tree*

Every nonterminal node represents an indefinitely large class of predicates, only a few of which are shown in the tree as examples. Thus the node with "is asleep" and "is hungry" would also contain "is awake" and "is frightened," among many other predicates. Similarly, terminal nodes represent indefinitely large classes of terms, so that, in addition to "man" and "girl," the node under "is honest" and "is sorry" would contain all terms that denote sentient beings.

Finally, nonterminal nodes also represent classes of terms, namely the supersets of all sets of terms under any such node. Thus, the node with the predicate "is heavy" represents the union of several classes of terms which forms a superordinate class consisting of all physical objects. The result is that every node in the tree represents a class of terms which in turn denotes members of a certain ontological category. Thus, isomorphic to the predicability tree is an ontological tree with a different ontological category at each node (Fig. 2).

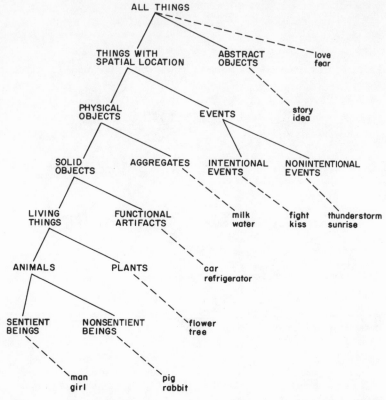

Figure 2.   *Ontological tree*

Sommers' theory is not a theory of selection restrictions, or restrictions on what lexical items can co-occur in a sentence, because the term "selection restrictions" has come to apply to a broader range of phenomena than is covered by his theory. For example, both "The bachelor is married" and "The idea is green" are commonly noted as violations of selection restrictions (cf. Leech, 1974), while only the latter sentence can be explained by Sommers' theory. To avoid any confusion, the anomalies of interest are referred to as "category mistakes," after Ryle.

Crucial to Sommers' theory is the idea that two predicates *A* and *B* cannot span intersecting sets of terms. Predicate *A* can span a superset or a subset of terms spanned by *B*, or the two predicates can have no terms in common, but they can never span terms in common and also have terms that just *A* spans and terms that just *B* spans. The converse is also true: two terms cannot be spanned by intersecting sets of predicates.

This principle can be translated into tree structures as "the M constraint." The M constraint means that a group of predicates or terms cannot form either an M- or a W-shaped tree. Sommers claims that whenever such M's or W's appear, they are artifacts caused by ambiguous terms and predicates (Fig. 3). In this diagram, the term "the bat" is ambiguous in the M, while the predicate "is rational" is ambiguous in the W. Thus, while it may seem as though both "is made by hand" and "was dead" span "the bat," actually they are spanning two different terms, "the baseball bat" and "the animal," which happen to have the same phonological shape. Similarly, the predicate "is rational" stands for two predicates, one being "is expressible as a fraction," the other being "having reason." Once these ambiguities are recognized, the M's and W's disappear.

The M constraint is not necessarily true. It is theoretically possible, for example, for a representation of predicability to be a partial lattice instead of a hierarchical tree (Fig. 4). The M constraint is therefore a proposed constraint on how humans think about the world. In linguistic theory, trees that honor the M constraint have been designated by other means. For example, Wall (1972) refers to a condition of "nontangling," while Bever and Langendoen (1971) refer to a "nonconvergence" constraint.

The M constraint can be seen as an attempt to satisfy partially the condition of explanatory adequacy. That is, of all the possible ways in which predicates and terms can be organized, only those organizations that obey the M constraint are psychologically natural. It may not be a sufficient condition for

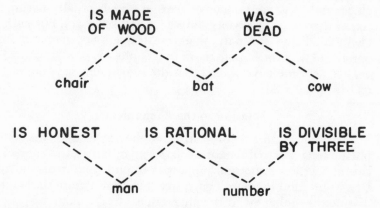

Figure 3. *Artifactual M and W structures resulting from ambigious terms and predicates*

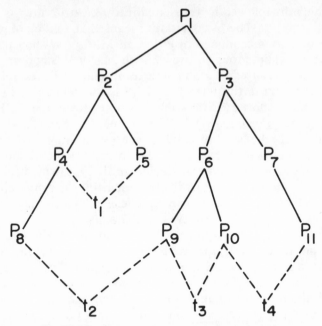

Figure 4.   *Hypothetical partial lattice incorporating M structures*

naturalness since other factors, such as contradictions, may also make certain predicate-term combinations non-natural.

At a deeper level, if the predicability tree is actually a reflection of the ontological tree, then the M constraint can be viewed as a partial attempt to put forth an explanatorily adequate theory of the knowledge structure of ontological categories. Only those structures that are organized as rigid hierarchies, and thus are nonconvergent, are conceptually natural. Again this would probably only be a necessary and not sufficient condition for naturalness. Although Sommers offers "proof" of why the M constraint must hold, the proof is controversial, as some have argued that the basic premise is not correct (Appendix A).

Relation to the Phenomena

The predicability theory can be applied to each of the four phenomena: anomaly, natural classes, similarity, and copredication. Certain structural properties of both the predicability tree (Fig. 1) and the ontological tree (Fig. 2) illustrate the same distinctions inherent in the phenomena.

With respect to anomaly, the tree marks the distinction between sensible and nonsensible predicates. A predicate may sensibly apply to a term if it dominates that term in a tree. For example, "the rock is heavy" is sensible; but "the secret is heavy" is not sensible since "the secret" is not dominated by "is heavy." The term "dominate" is used here in the traditional linguistic sense (cf. Wall 1972). A node x dominates a node y if there is a connected sequence of uniformly descending branches from x to y. A branch descends if it goes from a node closer to the unique "top" node of the tree to one of the many "bottom" nodes.

For a class to be natural, there must be some node in the tree that exhaustively dominates all and only the terms in that class. Conversely, non-natural classes are those classes that include terms on different branches but fail to include all terms that are common to those branches. For example, the class consisting of humans and plants is non-natural since it fails to include also nonhuman animals. This is because nonhuman animals are dominated by the node containing the predicate "is alive," which is the lowest predicate that spans both humans and plants. Another prediction made by the rule is that the only natural class which could include both birds and ideas would have to be the class of all things, since the lowest node that spans both of these terms is the topmost node in the tree.

This notion of naturalness should not be confused with other versions in the psychological literature. It is not concerned with the most natural member of a category, such as a robin being a better examplar of a bird than a penguin is; nor is it concerned with the most natural levels of thinking about classes, such as the basic level categories of Rosch (1973, 1974, 1976). Instead, this notion of natural categories is concerned with which sets of ontological classes can be collapsed into larger classes that also form coherent ontological wholes.

Similarity of classes also has a structural analogue in the predicability tree. Term classes that are closely dominated by a common predicate are more similar to each other than classes that are distantly dominated. For example, term classes t_1 and t_2 are more closely dominated than t_1 and t_3 if the lowest predicate common to t_1 and t_2 is dominated by the lowest predicate common to t_1 and t_3. Thus, in a tree illustrating similarity between classes (Fig. 5) term classes a and b are more similar to each other than are classes a and c since P_1, the lowest predicate common to a and b, is dominated by P_2, the lowest predicate common to a and c. The relation is also transitive. For example, if b is more similar to c than to d and a is more similar to b than to c, then a is more similar to c than to d.

This rule correctly predicts that humans are more similar to

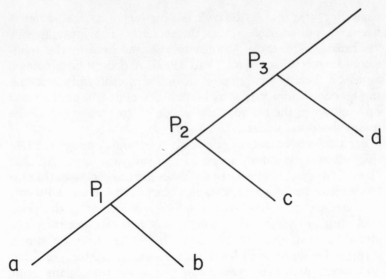

Figure 5. *Tree showing similarity of natural classes*

other animals than they are to plants, and that humans are more similar to plants than they are to events. It is essential that this rule apply to pairs *a-b* and *a-c*, not to pairs *a-b* and *c-d* where there is no shared class between the two pairs. As a result, the theory is unable to predict relative similarities between pairs, such as plants and humans versus events and liquids.

There is another prediction that, while superficially appealing, is incorrect. It states that class *d* of terms would be more similar to class *c* than to either class *a* or class *b*. Such a prediction is appealing in that it seems to be claiming that term classes which are further apart, as measured by the number of tree links between them, are less similar. However, study of the various sets of pairs around the tree shows that the prediction is incorrect. For example, it predicts that humans are less similar to events than plants are. Such a prediction does not seem correct.

A closer analysis reveals at least two reasons why the prediction is invalid. First, if similarity judgments are based on the number of predicate nodes that the two classes share, it is easy to see why humans and other animals are more similar than humans and chairs. The reason is that the former pair shares the predicate nodes "is tall," "is alive," and "is hungry," while the latter pair shares only "is tall." To make this judgment more analogous to other accounts of similarity judgments, one might say that humans share the features "physical object," "living," and "animal," while humans and chairs share only the feature "physical object." Yet humans and events share exactly the same predicates, or features, as plants and events; hence there should be no predictable difference in similarity between them. This is not to say that there might not be a similarity difference owing to other factors, just that this theory cannot predict a difference.

The second reason is that it is not always easy to tell whether class *a* is really "further" away from *c* than *d* is. This is because future nodes may be discovered that dominate *d* but which are dominated by the lowest node common to *d* and *a*. It could happen, for example, that a couple of new nodes would be discovered that result in animals actually being further away from plants than humans (Fig. 6). Examples of such nodes are shown in parentheses, "is a nice brute" being meant as a predicate that spans only nonhuman animals. Because it is difficult, if not impossible, to know when all nodes have been found, one could never be completely sure which term class was further away. Such additional nodes could have no effect on the first similarity rule, as one branch will always be higher than the other no matter how many other branches intervene.

The tree represents possible copredications in that those predicates which are either at the same node or on a common line to the top node of the tree are copredicable. Two predicates are on a "common line" if one dominates the other, that is, if it is possible to travel from one predicate to the other by always moving in the same vertical direction along the branches. Thus, in Figure 1, "is dead" and "is heavy" are on a common line since one can travel from "dead" to "heavy" by always going "upward." By contrast, "is dead" and "is an hour long"

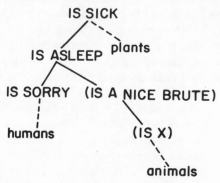

Figure 6.　*Tree showing possible future nodes*

are not on the same line since one has to travel both up and down to go between them. To use another example, "is honest" and "is sorry" are copredicable, as are "is honest" and "is red," but not "is honest" and "is an hour long."

In summary, a theory may be devised that apparently accounts for the four phenomena. The theory is most closely related to the work of Sommers, although aspects of it can be traced as far back as Aristotle. The theory extends Sommers' observations about predicability and ontological categories in three ways. First, it elaborates on the structure of the predicability tree by adding several more nodes. Second, it views the theory as posing a constraint on human cognition; in other words, the M constraint becomes a necessary condition for natural human concepts. Third, it posits that the structured knowledge of ontological categories is reflected in several different psychological phenomena.

Whereas Sommers discusses anomaly and to a lesser extent copredication, he does not treat them as psychological phenomena per se. He also does not mention other reflections of the ontological structure, such as natural class intuitions or similarity intuitions, and other possible phenomena, such as entailment. In general, Sommers appears to view his theory as a way of discovering ontological categories through predicability. In the theory presented here, the main emphasis concerns how the structured knowledge of ontological categories is reflected in various cognitive domains.

The proposed theory potentially makes a number of contributions to cognitive psychology. It puts a new emphasis on ontological knowledge and its link to language use and other conceptual processes. Ontological categories have a special status because they possess unique properties not shared with other sorts of conceptual categories. Thus, for example, much of the recent work by Rosch and her colleagues on natural categories presupposes and must presuppose the categories here.

The proposed theory explains several seemingly diverse phenomena with one unified account. Other work has generally treated phenomena such as selection restrictions as isolated cases and has failed to see the links to other phenomena, such as the link between similarity and natural classes via a common underlying knowledge base.

The theory posits a constraint on the form of natural concepts and, in so doing, begins to satisfy the goal of explanatory adequacy. In many respects, this satisfaction is the most important potential outcome, since it would yield helpful insights into what conceptual knowledge means and how that knowledge develops.

The proposed theory, if correct, offers a level of analysis at which rigid hierarchies, that is, those that are M-constrained, are psychologically illuminating. This level contrasts to the many other levels of analysis, such as truth functional, at which such hierarchies are not so successful. Rigid hierarchies are appealing, when psychologically valid, because of their simplicity and elegance as compared to cross-classification systems.

Finally, the proposed theory covers conceptual domains that have been of interest in developmental psychology. For example, the question of what sorts of things the child thinks there are in the world has been of considerable interest to Piaget. This theory may provide more specific and testable insights in an area that has previously been studied mostly in an anecdotal manner.

But all of these potentially positive benefits of the proposed theory are only promissory notes until the theory itself can be shown to account for the phenomena in a systematic fashion. Once that is done, it will be possible to reverse the procedure and use the phenomena to study the structure and development of ontological knowledge.

4 | Empirical Evaluation

I N THE EFFORT TO DETERMINE if the proposed theory is empirically correct, two questions must be asked. Do people have intuitions that suggest M-constrained trees? And if such trees are generated, are they the same for all individuals? Four experiments were designed to answer these questions, based on the underlying assumption that intuitions are an important source of empirical evidence. Experiments using the intuitions of others are necessary for a number of reasons, although cautions must be obeyed in using intuitions as psychological data.

On Using Intuitions

The first reason for conducting experiments on intuitions is that different adults might have different patterns of intuitions about anomaly, similarity, natural classes, and copredication that arise from different M-constrained representations. Some individuals might not even honor the M constraint at all. It is therefore necessary to determine the generality and uniformity of the phenomena across individuals.

The second and more important reason for conducting experiments on intuitions is that it is essential to demonstrate the reliability of techniques through which representations of ontological knowledge can be generated on the basis of natural language and other conceptual intuitions. Only if such techniques are successful with adults can they be modified for use with children whose intuitions are not necessarily the same.

It makes many psychologists uncomfortable to talk of using intuitions as psychological data since such mentalistic entities are often thought to be overly subjective and ephemeral. To a certain extent, this discomfort is legitimate; however, such discomfort should apply not to intuitions in general but rather to reliance on particular intuitions in specific tasks where they may not be appropriate. To be sure, if one desired to know the number of words in an individual's vocabulary, it would not be fruitful simply to ask that person to judge how many words he or she knew. Nonetheless, it would be foolhardy to deny all use of intuitions in psychology. If this were done, many of the established doctrines of psychophysics would no longer be accepted. A large number of classic studies in visual perception ask subjects to judge if "*x* is redder than *y*," if "*x* is brighter than *y*," and so forth. No one would want to discount such studies as meaningless.

Just as certain types of behavioral data can be reliable or unreliable, so can certain intuitions. The task is therefore not to establish the legitimacy of the use of intuitions, but rather to set up guidelines for their proper use as psychological data. Four guidelines have been developed, which serve as a general framework governing the use of intuitions rather than a set of strict principles.

First, it is desirable to have the intuitions easily accessible and fairly uniform across individuals. If subjects have to ponder for hours, or if they display markedly different patterns of answers, then the intuitions are less likely to be helpful. Gleitman and Gleitman (1977), in describing the use of intuitions in linguistic theory, illustrate how some linguistic intuitions are more easily accessible than others. Thus, intuitions about semantics, and to a lesser extent about grammar, are much more accessible than intuitions about phonology.

Second, intuitions must also concern highly specific, well-focused phenomena and not vague or amorphous ones. Otherwise different subjects may be giving intuitions about different things.

A third guideline is that of nontransparency. Intuitions are more convincing as psychological data when it is not immediately apparent to the subject how they fit into a theory. If the theory can be easily seen through the intuitions, there is the danger of introducing theoretical biases and general preconceptions as confounding factors.

Finally, intuitions are more convincing if there are independent ways of verifying their accuracy. One of the best ways to accomplish this is to use several different sets of intuitions and to show that they all converge to yield the same theory. In the present context, if intuitions about all four phenomena yield the same underlying tree representation, then they will provide not only strong evidence for the representation but also an excellent demonstration of the validity of each set of intuitions as a means for constructing a representation. These four guidelines should make it possible to judge whether the intuitions used in the studies of the four phenomena are appropriate forms of data.

The Study of Anomaly

Are subjects able to pick out certain sentences as anomalous, and are those sentences the same as ones predicted by an M-constrained tree? An experiment was performed to answer these questions.

Sixteen undergraduates and psychology graduate students were each given the following instructions:

> Some of the following sentences seem anomalous in that they just don't make any sense. Others make sense even though they may be either true or false. Thus, "The moon is purple" makes sense even

Table 1 *Stimulus sentences used in anomaly study*

The tree is tall.	The recess is thought about.
The girl is sorry.	The secret is asleep.
The water is dead.	The recess is tall.
The house is heavy.	The rabbit is asleep.
The tree is heavy.	The rabbit is heavy.
The house is tall.	The girl is heavy.
The girl is dead.	The rabbit is thought about.
The water is asleep.	The rabbit is dead.
The water is tall.	The rabbit is sorry.
The house is an hour long.	The tree is asleep.
The water is thought about.	The house is thought about.
The house is asleep.	The tree is thought about.
The water is sorry.	The recess is an hour long.
The water is an hour long.	The secret is tall.
The girl is thought about.	The water is heavy.
The secret is heavy.	The girl is an hour long.
The secret is dead.	The house is dead.
The tree is sorry.	The recess is sorry.
The girl is tall.	The house is sorry.
The recess is dead.	The tree is dead.
The rabbit is tall.	The secret is an hour long.
The girl is asleep.	The secret is thought about.
The secret is sorry.	The recess is asleep.
The tree is an hour long.	The rabbit is an hour long.
The resess is heavy.	

though it is false, but "Justice is purple" is just nonsense. You can imagine the moon being purple but you just can't imagine justice being purple without changing the essential meaning of "justice" or "is purple." To put it another way, you would know how to find out whether the moon was purple, but there is no way that you could find out whether justice is purple rather than some other color. If a metaphorical reading is the only one that makes a sentence acceptable, you should consider it anomalous since metaphors change the meanings of at least one of the words in the sentence. Please read over the sentences listed below several times and then put an "X" before each sentence that you think is anomalous, i.e., you just can't imagine it without changing the essential meaning(s) of one or more words in the sentence. If you think that any of the words are ambiguous, please make a note of it. Remember, if the only way that you have a sentence make sense is to use metaphor, then that sentence should be judged as anomalous.

The stimulus sheet contained forty-nine sentences (Table 1) representing every possible predicate-term pair in a simplified experimental tree (Fig. 7). This tree is a simplified version of the one shown in Figure 1 in that certain nodes have been de-

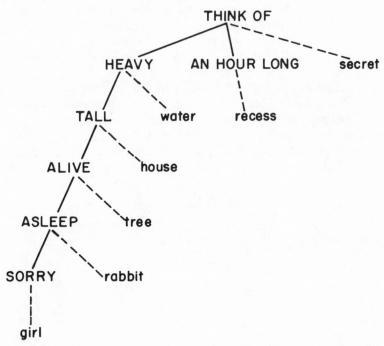

Figure 7. *Simplified predicability tree used in anomaly study*

leted in order to make the total number of sentences more manageable.

If one obtains intuitions about the sensibleness of all possible predicate-term pairs in a set, it is possible to construct a tree out of those intuitions. The procedure relies upon the fact that the tree represents various subsets of spanning relations. That is, if sentences Rx, Ry, Px, and Qy are all sensible and if sentences Py and Qx are anomalous, then one knows immediately that, if the M constraint is honored, R must dominate both P and Q in the tree as follows:

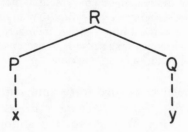

Sommers shows that if one assumes the M constraint, this rule must hold (Appendix A).

It may seem that, in order to construct the tree, one must assume that the subject honors the M constraint. In fact, this is not the case. There is a procedure for constructing a tree which illustrates how violations of the M constraint can be discovered.

Tabulate all responses by noting what terms are spanned by what predicates (Table 2). To construct a tree from such a table involves four steps. First, take the predicate that spans the largest set of terms and put it at the top node of the tree. If there are several predicates that span nonintersecting sets of terms which have no supersets, then there will be several trees with

Table 2 *Spanning relations showing no intersection of term sets and no M-constraint violation*

Terms Spanned	Predicate	Term
1	is sorry	1. girl
1, 4, 5, 7	is tall	2. secret
1, 4, 5	is alive	3. recess
3	is an hour long	4. rabbit
1, 4	is asleep	5. tree
1, 4, 5, 6, 7	is heavy	6. water
1, 2, 3 ,4, 5, 6, 7	is thought about	7. house

Table 3 *Spanning relations showing intersection of term sets and generation of M structure resulting from ambiguous predicate*

Terms Spanned	Predicate	Term
1	is sorry	1. girl
1, 4, 5, 7, 2	is tall	2. secret
1, 4, 5	is alive	3. recess
3	is an hour long	4. rabbit
1, 4	is asleep	5. tree
1, 4, 5, 6, 7	is heavy	6. water
1, 2, 3, 4, 5, 6, 7	is thought about	7. house

each of those predicates as top nodes. Sommers states that, in a natural language, there is always one predicate that spans all terms. Second, take the predicates that span the largest subsets of those sets of terms used in step 1 and put them at nodes directly under their respective supersets. Third, repeat the procedure in step 2 with predicates that span smaller and smaller subsets until there are no more predicates left. And fourth, if two predicates ever span exactly the same set of terms, then they are put at the same node. If this procedure is applied to Table 2, it yields the simplified experimental tree.

To see how this procedure can yield an M structure, or in this instance a W, consider the case in which "tall" is seen as ambiguous, meaning either "long vertical extent" or "unlikely" (Table 3). The table thus constructed differs from Table 2, which did not contain any intersecting sets of terms to the left of the predicates; the sets were either in superset-subset relations or they were nonintersecting. In Table 3, however, the sets of terms before "is tall" and "is heavy" intersect in the following manner:

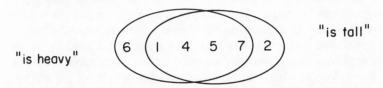

If the table were to contain any such intersecting sets of terms, and if the subject did not note the relevant ambiguity, the M constraint would be violated.

In this example a predicate is ambiguous. It is also possible to get an apparent M when a term is ambiguous (Table 4). In this case "the bee" refers to the insect or to a social event, such

Table 4 *Spanning relations showing intersection of term sets and generation of M structure resulting from ambiguous term*

Terms Spanned	Predicate	Term
1	is sorry	1. girl
1, 4, 5, 7	is tall	2. secret
1, 4, 5	is alive	3. recess
3, 4	is an hour long	4. bee
1, 4	is asleep	5. tree
1, 4, 5, 6, 7	is heavy	6. water
1, 2, 3, 4, 5, 6, 7	is thought about	7. house

as a spelling bee. As a result, there are several intersecting sets of terms:

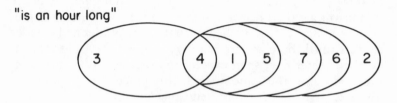

All of these intersections would vanish if the subject were to declare that "the bee" was ambiguous.

It should be apparent that not all ambiguities create M's. For example, "the bat" does not create an M in the simplified experimental tree because there is no special predicate that applies to the bat used in baseball and not to the bat that flies. Of course, there is such a predicate in the larger tree shown in Figure 1.

Intuitions from thirteen out of sixteen subjects resulted in trees that did not violate the M constraint. Ten of these trees were identical to the simplified experimental tree. Two of the remaining three subjects had trees that were the same as the simplified experimental tree except that "The rabbit is sorry" was taken as sensible. The one remaining subject generated a slightly unusual tree in which "house" was only spanned by "think of" and not "heavy" or "tall." This may have been a consequence of an ambiguity with "house." All other relations were identical to the experimental tree. One indication that the data support the theory comes from the fact that if an "average tree" were constructed by representing only those judgments that more than 80 percent of the subjects agreed upon, the entire experimental tree would be constructed.

Of the three M-constraint violators, two violated the M constraint only once; the other did so four times. Even with these violations, the data strongly support the theory. Of the many possible alternatives that could have occurred by chance, the predicted tree representation was the only real pattern observed. When a binomial expansion was used, these results were found to be significant at the .001 level, where the probability of generating a tree identical to the experimental tree was 1/249 for any given subject. The probability of generating *any* tree that obeyed the M constraint was also very low (Appendix 2).

The Study of Natural Classes

Do subjects have intuitions about what classes are natural and what classes are nonnatural? Also, are these classes predicted by the tree theory? A study was carried out to answer these questions.

Sixteen graduate and undergraduate students in psychology served as subjects. None of these subjects participated in the anomaly study. Each subject was given an instruction sheet and seven slips of paper, each of which named a class of terms and gave four examples of such terms; for example, liquids: milk, water, mercury, gasoline. The instructions were as follows:

This envelope contains seven slips of paper each of which stands for a class of things. Four examples of members of each class are given, but try to think of the class as a whole with all its members. Your task is to put together those classes that you think best go together to form a new class. You should do this in six steps, putting together first those two classes that you think best go together of all the seven classes. Then repeat this five more times until finally you have just one big class containing all seven initial classes. Always put together just two classes in any one step. Once you combine any two classes X and Y, *the resultant class* (X + Y) can also be combined with other classes. So if you think that three classes go together, you show it by combining two in one step (hopefully those two that go together best), e.g., X with Y and then combine the resultant class (X + Y) with Z. The whole process is illustrated in the following example where one is initially given the seven classes: dogs, cats, cows, pigs, bees, frogs, birds. One might combine them by the following six steps:

		Two classes combined	Possible reason
best	1.	dogs with cats	both pets
	2.	cows with pigs	both farm animals
	3.	(dogs + cats) with (cows + pigs)	both domesticated animals
	4.	bees with birds	both fly
	5.	(dogs + cats + cows + pigs) with frogs	both land animals
	6.	(dogs + cats + cows + pigs + frogs) with (birds + bees)	both are animals
worst			

go together

The possible reasons are given just to give you a feel for how to do the task. Different people may have different reasons and they may also have different sequences of combinations. There are two rules you must follow. 1. Once you combine two classes, they must stay combined as one new class, you can't separate them later. 2. You must go through all six steps until you reach just one big class even if the last couple of combinations don't seem very good at all. And remember to combine only two classes at a time. You should proba- bly go through the sequence several times with just the slips of paper until you are sure it is the one you like. Then write down the sequence in the six spaces provided below, just as was done in the example, using parentheses and "with" to designate a combination. You do not have to give reasons.

The order of all class collapses was recorded. The classes of terms used in the experiment may be shown in a tree (Fig. 8).

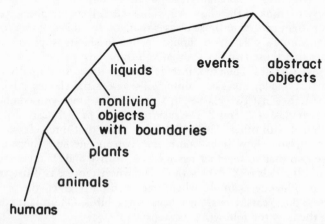

Figure 8. *Tree showing classes of terms used in natural classes study*

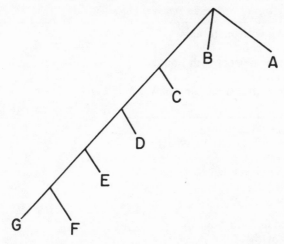

Figure 9. *Tree showing variants in ordering of collapses in natural classes study*

This tree is the same as the simplified experimental tree except that it has no predicates.

Analysis of the intuitions reveals that several different orderings could all be compatible with the same tree (Fig. 9). The first collapse could either be *B* with *A*, or *G* with *F*, or even *D* with *C*. Then, depending on which collapse is listed first, certain orders of other collapses are possible. In fact, thirty different orders are compatible with the schematic tree. This may seem like quite a few orders; however, the total number of possible orders for six collapses is greater than seven hundred. For this reason, any orders that correspond to the tree are unlikely to occur by chance.

As for the results, out of the sixteen subjects in the study, thirteen gave orders that were compatible with the tree shown in Figure 8. As the probability of giving a compatible order was less than 30/700, these results are significant at the .001 level, using a binomial expansion. The thirteen subjects showed several different correct orders (Table 5). The fact that there was some diversity in the orders actually strengthens the results as it suggests that the subjects were conforming precisely to what was predictable from the tree theory. If all the subjects gave just one order, then one might worry that the theory could only partially account for the phenomena since it allows thirty different orders.

Three subjects gave orders that disagreed with the tree

Table 5 *Correct orders in natural classes study*

1. humans with mammals
2. 1 with plants
3. nonliving objects with liquids
4. 2 with 3
5. events with abstract objects
6. 4 with 5

1. humans with mammals
2. plants with nonliving objects
3. 1 with 2
4. abstract objects with events
5. 3 with liquids
6. 4 with 5

1. mammals with humans
2. plants with 1
3. nonliving objects with liquids
4. 2 with 3
5. 4 with events
6. 5 with abstract objects

Table 6 *Incorrect orders in natural classes study*

1. humans with abstract objects
2. 1 with events
3. nonliving objects with liquids
4. 2 with mammals
5. 4 with plants
6. 5 with 3

1. humans with events
2. 1 with abstract objects
3. mammals with plants
4. 2 with 3
5. nonliving objects with liquids
6. 4 with 5

1. humans with abstract objects
2. mammals with plants
3. liquids with nonliving objects
4. 1 with events
5. 4 with 3
6. 5 with 2

(Table 6). There were apparently two reasons for these deviant trees. First, the subjects were thinking of complementary matchings as well as class inclusion relations. Therefore humans and events were put in the same class because humans often participate in events and not because they share many qualities with events. Second, the examples given for the events were unfortunately only those that included humans, such as recesses, vacations, or therapy sessions, and not other kinds of events such as thunderstorms. This characteristic certainly might have helped to bias the subjects. In fact, one of the three subjects even noted that there seemed to be two ways to form classes, depending on what criteria were used; the second way resulted in a correct order.

This study was not a test of the M constraint. Rather, it presupposed a hierarchical tree representation and was designed to determine if natural class intuitions were consistent with the simplified experimental tree structure. The results indicate that this was generally the case.

Moreover, the study did not use any predicates, and yet it produced orders that corresponded almost perfectly with the theory. This outcome is one of several pieces of evidence that the tree represents more than just a linguistic restriction on the co-occurrence privileges of predicates and terms.

The Study of Class Similarity

Do adults have intuitions about relative similarities between natural classes that are in accordance with the simplified experimental tree? A study was designed to answer this question.

Thirteen college undergraduates served as subjects in a group setting. None participated in the other studies. Each subject was given an envelope containing eleven slips of paper. Each slip of paper had two classes of terms on it, every class being represented by four examples as well as a general name for the whole class (Table 7).

The instructions were as follows:

You should all have envelopes containing eleven slips of paper. Please take out all the slips that have the class "humans" written on them. There are six slips of that type. Now each slip has two classes of things on it, for example humans and liquids, or humans and plants, or humans and ideas. Under each class name are four examples of members of that class. For example, under liquids are

Table 7   *Class pairs used as stimuli in class similarity study*

HUMANS	NONHUMAN MAMMALS
men, women, boys, girls vs.	dogs, pigs, cows, rabbits . . .
	PLANTS
	trees, flowers, grass, moss . . .
	NONLIVING OBJECTS
	rocks, houses, chairs, shoes . . .
	LIQUIDS
	water, milk, gasoline,
	mercury . . .
	EVENTS
	recesses, vacations, fights,
	meetings . . .
	ABSTRACT THINGS
	ideas, secrets, concepts,
	thoughts . . .
PLANTS	NONHUMAN MAMMALS
trees, flowers, grass, moss . . . vs.	dogs, pigs, cows, rabbits . . .
	NONLIVING OBJECTS
	rocks, houses, chairs, shoes . . .
	LIQUIDS
	water, milk, gasoline,
	mercury . . .
	EVENTS
	recesses, vacations, fights,
	meetings . . .
	ABSTRACT THINGS
	ideas, secrets, concepts,
	thoughts . . .

gasoline, water, milk, and mercury. What I want you to do is to think how similar the objects in the two classes on any slip are, and then order the six slips from the one that has the two classes that seem the most similar to the one that has the two classes that seem the most different. For example, you might take the slip with humans and plants and try to think if those two classes are more or less similar than, say, humans and liquids.

Now this is very important. I want you to think of all objects that you believe belong in the class and not just the four examples shown. Also, please judge the similarity between the objects themselves, not on the basis of any relations that the two classes may have with each other. Thus, the class consisting of boats is not very similar to the class of liquids because boats are not the same sorts of things as liquids even though these two classes have a very obvious relation to each other. To use another example, barking sounds are not very similar to dogs because sounds are not the same sorts of things as animals, even though of course dogs and their barks are intimately related. The point is, don't confuse similarity between classes of objects with the relations that exist between them. O.K., please go ahead and order the six slips.

[*After the six slips were ordered*] You now have five remaining slips, each of which has the class "plants" on it along with another class. Please order these five slips on the basis of similarity between the two classes on any slip.

All slips were randomized with respect to order; the order of mention of the two classes on any one slip was also randomized.

The reason for having two different ordering tasks was to see if two sets of intuitions, such as those for plants and humans, would both be forecast by the simplified experimental tree. This was a way of testing the generality of the theory's predictions about similarity.

The theory predicts that those classes which are more closely dominated by a common predicate will be more similar than those that are more distantly dominated. This prediction means that if a set of pairs $A-B$, $A-C$, $A-D$, $A-E$, and $A-F$ is ordered on the basis of similarity, they can be put into a hierarchical representation. For example, if A and B are judged to be more similar than A and C, the lowest node common to A and B will be dominated by the lowest node common to A and C.

While the intuitions gathered do not permit recreation of the original experimental tree, they do allow construction of analogous trees with which to make comparisons. The procedure consisted simply of constructing a node that dominated both humans and the class judged most similar to humans. The next step was to construct a node that dominated the first node and the class that was the next most similar to humans. This step was repeated until the class that was judged the least similar was dominated by a node. The same procedure was then performed with those classes that were judged to be similar to plants.

The trees that were constructed differed from the experimental tree in that, as the experiment required strict orders with no ties, each node could have only two subordinate branches. For this reason, the study forced subjects to put abstract things and events in dominance-subordinance relations to each other. Two trees were therefore the correct analogues to the predicability tree, one with events above abstract things and one with abstract things above events. In addition, the trees for humans, hereafter called "human" trees, differed from those for plants, hereafter called "plant" trees, in that the latter omitted the node for humans (Figs. 10–11)

Nine out of thirteen subjects had intuitions that generated perfect human trees and nine out of thirteen had intuitions that generated perfect plant trees. These results are significant

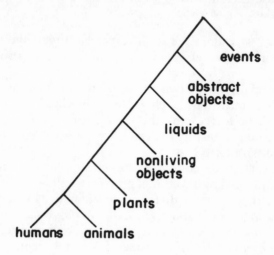

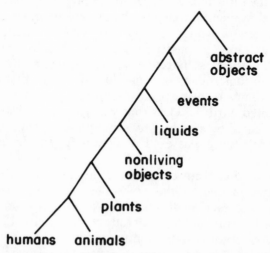

Figure 10. *Possible orderings of human trees in class similarity study*

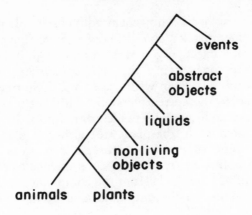

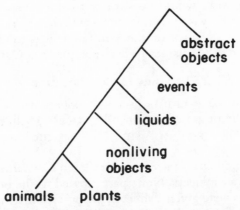

Figure 11. *Possible orderings of plant trees in class similarity study*

at the .001 level, using binomial expansion, as the odds that a given subject would construct a correct order by chance were 2/720 for human trees and 2/120 for plant trees.

Of the four subjects who generated incorrect human trees, two made only one error, consisting of switching the order of adjacent classes. One subject switched the order of nonliving objects and plants, while the other switched the order of liquids and nonliving objects. The other two subjects judged events and abstract objects as being very similar to humans, which seems to be the same sort of error noted in the natural classes study where humans and events were sometimes collapsed together. Even with the errors, the trees are still quite similar to the correct versions.

Of the four subjects who generated incorrect plant trees, all made only one mistake, consisting of an inversion of adjacent classes. Three subjects inverted the order of liquids and nonliving objects, and one reversed the order of nonliving objects and nonhuman animals. Even with the errors, these trees were all quite similar to the correct versions. Three of these subjects were the same subjects who made errors for the human trees. The fact that none of the plant tree errors involved abstract things and events supports the argument that errors with these classes in the human tree were a consequence of mistakenly judging similarity on the basis of the complementary relations between humans, on the one hand, and events and abstract things, on the other.

This study, like the study of natural classes, presupposed the M constraint and was a test of whether trees constructed under this assumption would be similar to the predictability tree. The similarity was shown to be very high, and this result was independent of whether the similarity was judged between humans and other classes or between plants and other classes.

The Study of Copredication

Do adults have intuitions about copredication that correspond to the proposed predicability tree? Do these intuitions honor the M constraint? A study was designed to answer these questions.

Sixteen graduate students and research assistants in psychology served as subjects. None participated in the other studies. All subjects were given a sheet of paper with instructions and a list of forty-five predicate pairs (Table 8). The subjects were instructed to try to think of anything that each pair of predicates could apply to. If they could think of such a thing, they were to write down its name. They were also cautioned to avoid all metaphors and to make a note of any predicates that they thought were ambiguous.

The instructions were as follows:

On the lower part of this sheet are forty-five pairs of predicates. Your task is to examine each pair of predicates and decide if both of them could apply to some thing. Please look at only the most literal meanings of the predicates; that is, don't use any metaphors. Thus, "is wilted" should apply only to plants. If you can't think of anything that two predicates could apply to, put an "X" next to that predicate pair (there are supposed to be several such cases). If there is something that both predicates apply to, write down an example

Table 8 *Stimuli used in copredication study*

is thought about and is heavy
is tall and is heavy
blooms and is thought about
blooms and leaks out of boxes
is heavy and is about a princess
is about a princess and is tall
is heavy and is an hour long
is broken and is thought about
leaks out of boxes and is heavy
is thought about and leaks out of boxes
is broken and is alive
is tall and is alive
is asleep and blooms
is about a princess and is asleep
is alive and is an hour long
leaks out of boxes and is an hour long
is thought about and is an hour long
is an hour long and is asleep
is heavy and is broken
is thought about and is alive
is alive and blooms
is broken and is about a princess
is broken and is an hour long
blooms and is broken
blooms and is tall
is heavy and is alive
is about a princess and is an hour long
is alive and is about a princess
is asleep and leaks out of boxes
is asleep and is thought about
is an hour long and is tall
leaks out of boxes and is about a princess
blooms and is about a princess
is asleep and is tall
blooms and is heavy
is broken and is tall
leaks out of boxes and is broken
is alive and is asleep
is tall and is thought about
blooms and is an hour long
is asleep and is heavy
is asleep and is broken
leaks out of boxes and is tall
is alive and leaks out of boxes
is about a princess and is thought about

of such a thing next to the predicate pair. If you think that any predicates are ambiguous, please make a note of it. Consider the following two examples. The predicate pair "is ungrammatical and is a prime number" receives an "X" since there is nothing that can be both ungrammatical and a prime number. The predicate pair "is green and is sorry" is O.K. since one can imagine something that could be green and feel sorry. Next to the pair one should write something like "a green humanoid" as an example of something to which both predicates apply. Note that even though a green humanoid is science fiction, one is still using the literal meanings of green and sorry. It is legitimate to imagine fictional objects as long as you don't change the meanings of the predicates. Also be careful that you don't have a hidden ambiguity in the name of the thing that you pick. Thus, while it may seem that "is sunny" and "is democratic" both apply to Italy, actually "is sunny" applies to a piece of land, while "is democratic" applies to a political system. The point is, Italy is ambiguous here. These two predicates really don't seem to have any one thing that they both apply to and should receive an "X". Please do this task on your own and don't compare your intuitions with those of others.

A judgment was incorrect if two predicates were considered copredicable when they were not on the same line to the top node of the simplified experimental tree.

The vast majority of judgments were in accordance with the theory and did not violate the M constraint. Even when ambiguities are included as deviations from the theory, the average was only 3.4 incorrect out of all 45 judgments per subject. These results are significant at the .001 level, using binomial expansion.

No subject gave responses that were in exact accordance with the simplified experimental tree. This was apparently a consequence of the fact that some of the predicates were interpreted in a different manner than was intended by the experimenter. In particular, the predicate "is broken," which was supposed to mean "is defective," was for the most part interpreted as "is fractured." In addition, several subjects who took "is broken" to mean "is fractured" nevertheless did not think that something which "was asleep" could be broken. This pattern of responses appeared to cause a violation of the M constraint, but questioning of these subjects revealed that the violation was probably not genuine. The subjects stated either that "is broken" spanned all physical objects or just inanimate objects. In the latter case, they agreed that if "broken" applied just to inanimate objects, then plants were alive in a very dif-

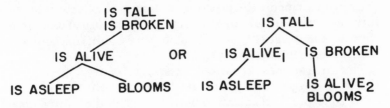

Figure 12.   *Trees showing intuitions in copredication study*

ferent sense from animals. It therefore seems that the subjects'
intuitions correspond to one of two tree fragments (Fig. 12).

The other major deviation from the simplified experimental
tree was that twelve of the sixteen subjects felt that "is about a
princess" and "is an hour long" were copredicable of things
like movies and television shows. To find out whether these
subjects had overlooked ambiguities in the names of the objects they had selected, seven of the subjects were later asked if
various paraphrases of their responses could also take both
predicates. The two paraphrases for "the movie" were "the
plot or theme of the movie" and "the showing of the movie."
All seven subjects agreed that the thing denoted by the first
paraphrase could only be about a princess and could not have
duration while the second paraphrase denoted things that
could only have duration and not be about something. All subjects also agreed that the paraphrases were accurate restate-
ments of the original term "the movie" in context. These follow-up results lend support to the claim that an ambiguity
caused the apparent collapse of these two categories.

This study seemed to prompt the subjects more toward the
use of ambiguities than the previous three. Perhaps the chal-
lenge of trying to think of at least one thing to which the two
predicates could apply is the cause of the bias. Subjects were
unwilling to fail to come up with something. This reluctance
may explain why in no instance a subject said that two predicates were not copredicable when the theory predicted that
they were.

Methodological Issues

These four studies empirically verify the generality of each
of these four phenomena of anomaly, natural classes, similarity, and copredication. They also show that the four phenomena are in accord with the theory of predicability. The
studies thus represent four different pieces of evidence that

converge to support the proposed theory. It is evident that the intuitions used are legitimate forms of psychological data since they appear to satisfy the criteria of accessibility, specificity, nontransparency, and convergence.

The three studies on natural classes, similarity, and copredication all suggest that the predicability tree relfects an underlying conceptual organization of the world. In the natural class and similarity studies, subjects were asked to think of the objects themselves and how they were related. Admittedly the objects were designated by linguistic means, but there was little doubt that the subjects were thinking of the objects and not just of the words that denoted them. In the copredication task, the subjects were asked to think of an object that satisfied both predicates, and informal reports indicated that subjects were trying to imagine various objects and not just semantic relations. While none of these studies provides conclusive evidence for a conceptual framework as the underlying origin of the predicability tree, they all point in that direction.

One might argue that the tree is represented in a language-specific way but at a deeper level than surface utterances or actual lexical items. Such an argument has the burden of showing how such a representation would differ from other types of cognitive representation and how it would be a more suitable source of the predicability tree. It might be argued that those categories which can be used in a semantic representation are a subset of all categories that can be used in other cognitive domains, and that the subset honors the M constraint. Such a proposal is unlikely, however, in light of what seems to have occurred in the studies. The subjects were asked if they could "conceive" of anything that satisfied certain properties, a word that suggests a broader range of mental operations than those that are solely linguistic.

The notion of the existence of a conceptual structure underlying the linguistic level makes the theory more complete. It helps to explain the apparent violations of the M constraint. If natural languages are fraught with ambiguities, it is not surprising that a linguistic measure of the tree should yield some apparent violations. This is not to say that nothing could disconfirm the tree, but rather that evidence which relies on language should be scrutinized for any hidden ambiguities to which a speaker of that language would agree after careful reflection.

It might be objected that the studies on anomaly and copredication are actually just measures of empirical knowledge about the world. That is, it could be that all responses were made simply on the basis of whether or not it was true that a predicate applied to some object. Perhaps the most convincing argument against this proposal is that many of the objects listed in the copredication study, among which were Rip Van Winkle, King Kong, a broken Empire State Building, a giant flower, and a giant person, do not exist in the real world. Another argument against the proposal that empirical knowledge was the basis for the judgments is that the results of the anomaly and copredication studies are so similar to those of the similarity and natural class studies, and the subjects' responses in the latter studies clearly could not have been based on judgments of empirical truth.

The subjects' responses in all four experiments might have been strongly influenced by their recognition of the hierarchical organization implicit in the stimuli. But in fact this happened rarely. After each experiment, the goals of the research were explained to any subject who would listen. Most subjects were surprised when they were shown the underlying hierarchical organization, for they had not been "cued in" to the hierarchies by knowing the theory in advance.

The four studies lead to four conclusions. First, there are strikingly few individual differences between adults in intuitions concerning all four phenomena. Intuitions by different subjects generally yielded the same tree representations. Second, there are reliable and workable techniques for constructing tree representations on the basis of intuitions about the phenomena.

Third, the data converge; that is, intuitions about four different phenomena almost invariably resulted in the same underlying tree. This finding not only provides evidence for the intuitions as reliable and objective forms of data but also supports the claim that there is a common aspect of knowledge underlying and responsible for the four phenomena. Finally, the patterns of intuitions were in conformity with the theory, not only because they converged on the same structure, but also because that structure honored the M constraint.

5 | Other Psychological Research

I T HAS BEEN SHOWN that a theory of ontological knowledge accounts for and is empirically compatible with the four phenomena of anomaly, natural classes, similarity, and copredication. The question remains, however, whether the theory relates to other psychological and linguistic research. It is important to determine to what extent the theory is supported by other work. Moreover, such a comparison will put the theory in an appropriate context and will clarify its significance.

Semantic Memory Research

It may seem that research on semantic memory (e.g. Collins and Quillian, 1969; Loftus, 1977) is closely related to the theory of ontological knowledge because of mutual references to tree structures. However, similarities are more apparent than real, because these two areas proceed at different levels of investigation. Semantic memory research usually proceeds at the level of truth values, while research on ontological knowledge proceeds at the level of possibility. Some of the early work at the truth-value level even employed hierarchical tree representations. Collins and Quillian, for example, proposed truth-dependent trees similar to the one shown in Figure 13.

Such a tree can be modified to make it more analogous to Sommers' trees by putting all predicates that truthfully apply to a group of objects at the same node (Fig. 14). This modification does not contradict the Collins and Quillian proposal; at worst it can be regarded as an oversimplification because it obliterates the distinction between properties and class names by putting them all at the same node. Loftus (1977) argues that

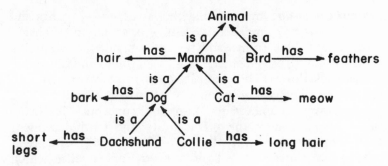

Figure 13. *Truth-dependent tree*

such a distinction is important, but for purposes of comparison it is not essential.

This general type of tree is very different from the predicability tree. One difference is that it makes many more distinctions than a predicability tree, such as dachshunds as opposed to collies. In fact, the truth-dependent tree can grow endlessly downward as one learns more and more about the world. A second difference is that representations of semantic knowledge as hierarchies based on truth values do not honor the M constraint. Indeed, a great many alternative truth-dependent trees can apply to exactly the same set of objects. For example, one

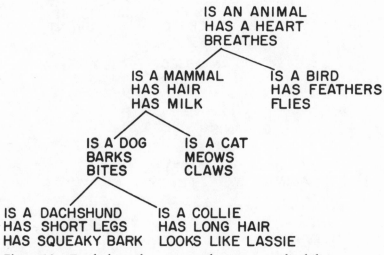

Figure 14. *Truth-dependent tree analogous to predicability tree*

can put caviar and emeralds together as expensive things and tar and cabbages as inexpensive things, or caviar and cabbages together as edible things and tar and emeralds as nonliving things, or cabbages and emeralds as green things and caviar and tar as black things. The predicability tree, however, can classify a group of objects only one way; otherwise it would violate the M constraint and create non-natural concepts. This situation illustrates how the predicability and truth-dependent trees are representing very different sorts of things. The predicability tree represents the basic categories of existence, which is the reason those categories are called "ontological." In contrast, the truth-dependent tree represents any true distinctions that can be made about the world. While a truth-dependent tree can be made to represent ontological categories (Fig. 15), it is just one of an indefinitely large class of truth-dependent trees. For these reasons, predicability trees and truth-dependent trees turn out to have very different psychological properties.

The original 1969 Collins and Quillian model has been subject to a variety of criticisms. For example, their model predicted that the number of hierarchical links separating a category name from one of its properties was related to the

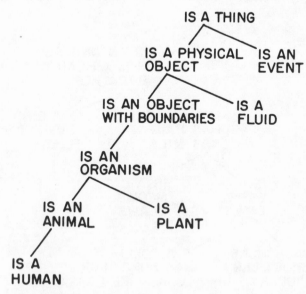

Figure 15. *Truth-dependent tree representing ontological categories*

verification time of a sentence about the category name and property. However, Conrad (1972) and Smith, Shoben, and Rips (1974) have demonstrated that Collins and Quillian confounded the number of links between a noun concept and its property with the strength of associative relatedness between a noun and its property. With proper controls, verification time is strongly correlated with associative strength and not with the number of links. However, Collins and Loftus (1974) have since argued that their so-called theory of "cognitive economy" was misinterpreted and that Conrad was not testing their claim. A second objection to the 1969 Collins and Quillian work is that it failed to explain why some members of a category can be verified faster than others (Rosch, 1973).

Because of these objections, more recent models almost invariably incorporate devices to account for associative relatedness and typicality effects (cf. Smith, 1977). As a consequence, these models are even less closely related to the predicability tree. For example, the marker search model of Glass and Holyoak (1975) contains a hierarchical structure in which links are very similar to Katz's (1972) redundancy rules, where one semantic marker implies another, such as avian → animate. This in itself could actually have interesting relations to the predicability tree, and in fact, Katz's redundancy rules recreate the predicability tree in many respects, though not precisely. However, in an attempt to account for associative relations and typicality, Glass and Holyoak also include certain "shortcut" links which violate the hierarchical structure and create all sorts of M structures. Similarly, later versions of the Collins and Quillian theory include new features that do away with simple hierarchies (e.g. Collins and Loftus, 1975; Loftus, 1977). And other models of semantic memory that are based on comparison of semantic features do not make any explicit use of hierarchical trees (e.g. Smith et al., 1974).

In sum, the theory of ontological knowledge is substantially different from most research in semantic memory. It does not contradict this research so much as it addresses different issues. Even where semantic memory research has emphasized simple hierarchical tree representations, the parallels are weak, for one set of trees is constructed on the basis of truth values while the other set is constructed on the basis of sense. Moreover, the recent trend has been away from such simple hierarchies toward tree structures or set theoretic models that are not at all like M-constrained hierarchical trees.

Natural Categories

Much of the recent work on semantic memory has relied extensively on theories about the structure of natural categories. The principal investigator in this area is Rosch, who has explored the structure of natural categories from several perspectives (Rosch, 1973, 1974; Rosch and Mervis, 1975; Rosch et al., 1976). Since the predicability tree demarcates ontological categories, those categories would seem to be related to Rosch's categories. However, as in the case of semantic memory research, the two types of categories are at different levels, and relations between them are somewhat indirect.

The categories that Rosch discusses are generally at a much "finer" level than those represented by the predicability tree. For example, Rosch devotes considerable attention to so-called "basic level categories," categories whose members have a large number of salient attributes in common and which are easy to distinguish from other categories. Examples of these categories would be tables, chairs, and beds. However, these three categories are all just part of one ontological category roughly corresponding to artifacts. It would be convenient to conclude, therefore, that Rosch's categories and ontological categories are not contradictory or incompatible but are simply different; that is, that they are correct but involve different levels of analysis. To a certain extent this is true, but it fails to reflect important interactions between the two that raise potential disagreements.

Consider, for example, Rosch's view of "family resemblances." She criticizes the notion that decisions about category membership are dichotomous. Instead, she argues, many natural categories are analog in nature, so that members vary along a "goodness" of membership continuum. This view gives rise to the notion that there is an ideal prototypical member of the category and that members who are closer to this prototype are the better members.

Superordinate semantic categories, according to Rosch, "are of particular interest because they are sufficiently abstract and have few, if any, attributes common to all members . . . although it is always possible for the ingenious philosopher or psychologist to invent criterial attributes . . . actual subjects rate superordinate categories as having few, if any, attributes common to all members" (pp. 576–577). Rosch's claim about superordinate categories would appear to have a direct bearing on ontological categories, for if it is true that more superordinate categories have few or no common attributes, then this should be especially the case for the highly superordinate ontological categories.

To strengthen her claims that superordinate classes have few criterial attributes and to gain insight into the internal structure of such classes, Rosch conducted an experiment in which college students were asked to list those "characteristics and attributes that people feel are common to and characteristic of" various objects, such as articles of clothing, types of furniture, or vehicles. Each of these superordinate categories had twenty members, varying along a continuum from "good" members, such as chairs as furniture, to "poor" members, such as telephones as furniture. Each subject had to list attributes that were characteristic of six items, which had been drawn by the experimenter from the six superordinate categories. Instructions called for attributes simply of the member objects, with no mention of the superordinate categories. The results were straightforward. While the subjects listed a number of attributes for each member of a category, they listed very few, if any, attributes as common to all members of the category. And on occasions when just one attribute was used, it was often not true of only that category, such as "You eat it" for fruit.

Yet these results do not prove that high-level natural categories have few, if any, criterial attributes. In fact, Rosch's tasks are open to an alternative interpretation in this respect, as they are in others (Armstrong et al., forthcoming). Although she concludes otherwise, her subjects were most likely well aware of numerous attributes that are common to all items in the superordinate categories, but which they did not immediately list owing to certain aspects of the specific task assigned. That is, Rosch's subjects presupposed certain attributes as given and then proceeded to list others. Thus, when subjects were asked to list characteristics of a particular vegetable, they did not tend to list features like "is a plant," "has cells," "has roots," or "grows." Nor did they list any features also common to a superordinate category, such as for physical objects, "has mass," "has volume," or "has a rigid structure." It seems that the subjects inferred from the instructions that they should give attributes appropriate for distinguishing a particular member from other members of the same class. But simply because they did not list high-level features, does not mean that subjects did not think vegetables had such attributes. In fact, informal inquiries of several colleagues reveal that, if asked to list "very basic" attributes common to vegetables, they will eventually list common features. Another reaction is that, after first failing to list such common attributes and then being asked if "is a plant" or "has mass" are common attributes, subjects will usually respond, "Of course those are common attributes, but I didn't think that was what you wanted," or "Those are so basic, I just assumed I shouldn't mention them."

The reason such elementary features are omitted in Rosch-type tasks is complicated, but it seems to be related to the task of giving definitions. The parallel becomes more apparent when definitions are viewed as lists of criterial features. If asked to define a butcher, one does not begin by saying "a physical object with mass, capable of growth"; rather, one lists those features that differentiate butchers from other members of the same ontological category. Thus, a dictionary definition of butcher is "a retail or wholesale dealer in meat" (Random House), or "one who slaughters animals and dresses their flesh" (Webster's). A definition gives those features that distinguish between butchers, bakers, and candlestick makers, not features that distinguish between butchers and glasses of milk. Some definitions may start off with a general word that cues one into the relevant ontological category, but definitions never go further to list the features of that ontological category or of more superordinate ones. Thus, a definition for "rutabaga" might start off with "a plant having" and then list various turniplike features, but would never list general physical object features. This distinction between definitional and ontological features should not be confused with the distinction drawn by Smith, Shoben, and Rips (1974) between defining and characteristic attributes. Although related, the two distinctions are not the same.

The point is that some features are so basic to categories that they are not even mentioned in descriptions of members of those categories. However, the fact that they are not always mentioned in no way proves that they are not psychologically real or important. Nor does it imply that the difference between the two types of features is unimportant.

Some of the categories used by Rosch raise a further problem. While it is true that categories such as fruits and vegetables may have few, if any, criterial features, it is also true that the more superordinate categories, such as plants, have a large number of unique criterial features. Thus, it is not necessarily the case that the more superordinate the category, the fewer criterial features it must have.

These observations suggest that ontological categories have

special properties all their own with respect to features. All members of such categories have certain fixed features in common. Moreover, there are several features that uniquely specify each ontological category, even though this may not be true for subordinate categories, at least as far down as basic-level categories. In addition, the fact that each category seems to possess a set of fixed attributes undermines many of the arguments for the necessity of prototypes. This does not mean that prototypes are unimportant or unnecessary to categories at other levels, but simply that they do not do much theoretical work at the ontological level. Nor does this deny that one hundred subjects might have some weak consensus about what a prototypical physical object consists of; it simply raises questions about how important that fact would be. Similarly, the fact that some subjects pick the number thirteen as the prototypical prime number does not mean that they think it is a "better" member of the class of prime numbers than "five" is (Armstrong et al., forthcoming).

In sum, Rosch's work should not be taken as yielding a complete account of the internal structure of all natural categories. While some categories may have features organized in a prototypical fashion, there are also other essential features that all members of any natural category must have. These features demarcate an ontological category that is either superordinate or equivalent to the category under investigation. It also appears that for Rosch's subjects essential features often are presupposed and, in many tasks, are not mentioned as defining attributes. These facts open some of Rosch's conclusions to reinterpretation. For example, it is not the case that the superordinate class "furniture" has no psychologically important features common to all members; rather, certain features pertaining to ontological categories are not normally accessed by subjects in Rosch's tasks. The point is not that the family resemblance or prototype view of category structure is completely mistaken, for such a view will clearly play an important role in a comprehensive account of natural categories. Rather, the point is that there appear to be two types of features which specify the internal structure of semantic categories and that only one type conforms to a family resemblance model.

In other work on natural categories the categories studied appear to be more similar to ontological ones. In the anthropological literature, Berlin et al. (1973) have described a level called the "unique beginner level." They propose that organisms are "grouped into a small number of classes known as taxonomic ethnobiological categories." These categories are hierarchically embedded in each other, with the topmost unique-beginner level involving such distinctions as animals and plants. Basic-level terms are at the third level down from the top, the "generic level." While the comparison between unique-beginner categories and ontological categories is difficult to make because of differing assumptions, it helps to illustrate the different levels of analysis and the special properties that categories at each level might have.

Anomaly

Anomaly plays an important role in the theory of ontological knowledge. Predicates that are combined with terms which they do not dominate form anomalous sentences. There have been a number of psychological studies of anomaly, which it is important to relate to the theory. The problem in reviewing the literature on anomaly, however, is that anomaly is frequently taken to denote a wider class of phenomena than category mistakes. For example, several investigators of selection restrictions lump together direct contradictions, such as the round square or the married bachelor, with anomalies. The focus here will be on those parts of the literature that deal with category mistakes.

Anomalous sentences have generally been shown to be a distinguishable class of sentences with special psychological properties. For example, Miller and Isard (1963) found that anomalous sentences are more difficult to perceive through noise than sensible sentences are, while Marks and Miller (1964) showed that anomalous sentences are more difficult to remember. Later investigators have repeatedly supported these findings, using a variety of techniques ranging from sorting procedures to reaction times (Epstein, 1969, 1972; Meyer, 1970; Steinberg, 1970). Such findings are obviously compatible with the claim that such anomalous sentences should be accorded a special status.

Some results, however, are at odds with the view of anomalous sentences as nonsensical and truth-valueless. Steinberg (1970a, 1972) has argued that while anomalous sentences are distinguishable from other sentences, they do have truth values; that is, they are false. He presents evidence that subjects rate anomalous sentences as false and their negations as true. But his method of negation has problems in that the simple insertion of a "not" makes it unclear whether the negations are a denial of a predicate's applicability to a term or a denial of the truth of the sentence. For example, "The rock is not honest" could mean either "It is not possible for the rock to be honest" or "The rock is dishonest." Sommers (1976) points out the same ambiguity. However, there are ways in which the ambiguity can be avoided, and in those cases subjects declare that both a sentence and its negation are deviant.

A more serious objection to the claim that anomalous sentences are nonsensical comes from Pollio and Burns (1977), who argue that all such sentences are interpretable. They claim that even when subjects take anomalous sentences literally, they are able to find sensible interpretations by constructing the appropriate contexts. Several reasons are possible for these results. First, many of the anomalies used by Pollio and Burns apparently were not true category mistakes. For example, the sentence "A bird has raised up gray neighbors" does not seem to mix categories on different branches. Thus, what Pollio and Burns define as anomalous may not be true category mistakes. Second, Pollio and Burns told subjects that the sentences they were going to hear had been usèd at some time in the past in rock music, poetry, political speeches, and the like. These instructions seem to have had the effect of urging the subject to use metaphor. Third, in the cases where subjects were able to interpret the sentences literally, there is the strong possibility that they were relying on extensive ellipses. For example, the sentence "She charged them by sweet hats" was interpreted as a suffragette's attack on a group of men while wearing a hat, which suggests that the subject was putting a heavy gloss on the original sentence. Subjects also used the strategy of making certain words technical terms, which gave them new meanings. Finally, subjects appeared always to have the option of adding a phrase like "He dreamed that," which makes any grammatical sentence acceptable. In sum, it should not be surprising that subjects can force an acceptable interpretation onto anomalous sentences. The real issue is whether they normally consider such sentences to be anomalous when they are not using such strategies.

While these studies of anomaly connect only tangentially with the theory of ontological knowledge, there is one other study that bears directly on the theory. In fact, the results of that study can be predicted by the theory. The study was conducted by Clark and Begun (1971) and was concerned with certain patterns of anomaly intuitions.

Clark and Begun considered three ways in which different types of subjects might interact with various types of predicates. First, all verbs could belong to mutually exclusive categories such that only one class was appropriate with one set of subjects and another class with a different set. Second, verbs could belong to hierarchical categories. "All verbs would be acceptable with human subjects, a subset of these would be acceptable with inanimate concrete subjects; a subset of the latter would be acceptable with abstract subjects." Or third, there could be a mixture of these two possibilities.

Two studies were conducted. In the first, subjects were told to rate, on a seven-point scale, the acceptability of a variety of subject-predicate combinations, such as human subject with animal predicate or abstract subject with human predicate. In the second study, subjects were requested to substitute a word in a sentence so that the substitution made better sense than the original. Both studies provide strong support for the view that verbs belong to a hierarchically arranged set of semantic categories ranging from humans to animals to concrete objects to abstract things.

What is especially striking about these studies is that Clark and Begun's theory and results are compatible with the theory of ontological knowledge. The subject-transitive verb compatibility is a special case of predicability and the general predicability tree embodies a hierarchical arrangement very similar to that proposed by Clark and Begun. In fact, by using the predicability tree, one is able to predict virtually all of Clark and Begun's results. The predicability tree is actually evidence for the third hypothesis, since some verbs do belong to mutually exclusive categories, such as "is red" versus "is ungrammatical," as well as being part of a hierarchical array. Clark and Begun simply did not happen to use such pairs, although they did mention that the final model is most likely to be a mixed model. It therefore seems that the Clark and Begun research can be incorporated easily into the proposed theoretical framework and actually used as a form of support.

Anomaly has also been studied by Alker (1966) to test Sommers' proposal that any predicates or terms which violate the tree structure must be ambiguous. For example, if both "The chair is hard" and "The problem is hard" are considered sensible, then "is hard" should be considered ambiguous. Alker's four different measures of ambiguity support Sommers' proposal. This, then, is a preliminary form of support for the M constraint, which is the basic component in Sommers' theory.

In sum, much of the prior research on semantic anomaly has not been sufficiently fine-grained to have a direct bearing on the theory of ontological categories. In addition, investigators have usually treated anomaly as an isolated phenomenon and have not seen it in a broader context as one of several manifestations of a deeper underlying knowledge. In those studies where a more detailed analysis of anomaly intuitions was made, the results and conclusions were consistent with the theory proposed.

Possible Lexical Items

The question arises why some words seem quite reasonable while others seem incomprehensible or at least highly unnatural. That is, new lexical items are either possible or impossible, if "possible" is used in the sense of humanly possible or conceptually natural. The predicability tree may help to explain this phenomenon and conforms with an analysis of possible lexical items by Bever and Rosenbaum (1971).

The authors contrast possible lexical items, such as "ogg," meaning the dead remains of an entire plant, to "triffid," meaning a plant that moves and communicates. They refer to "ogg" as an accidental lexical gap and to "triffid" as a systematic gap. What they mean by this distinction is that the lack of a word like "ogg" is just an accident of the English language, whereas the absence of a word like "triffid" is a consequence of some systematic way in which semantic knowledge is organized. They posit a hierarchy of semantic features to explain the difference between systematic and accidental gaps. Such hierarchies are also meant at least partially to explain selection restrictions and metaphors.

Bever and Rosenbaum argue that hierarchies must be nonconvergent. Moreover, they view this requirement as a psychological constraint and not a consequence of physical facts. "Thus it is not 'reality' which disallows convergences of lexical hierarchies, but the non-convergent property of the lexical system itself" (p. 597). This emphasis on nonconvergence, especially as a psychological property, is clearly related to the M constraint. The parallel is not complete, however, since the lexical hierarchies are based on true-false distinctions rather than predicability. This difference forced Bever and Rosenbaum to argue that there are several distinct lexical hierarchies. In fact, reflection reveals that there would be an enormous number of such hierarchies.

The predicability tree can account for the difference between accidental and systematic gaps if it is assumed that semantic features can be represented in terms of natural language predicates, an assumption that is commonly made and has proven to be useful in semantic analysis (Katz, 1972). Given this assumption, possible lexical items are those items whose features correspond to predicates that are copredicable. Thus "oggs" are possible items since their features correspond to predicates which span plants. In contrast, "triffids" are impossible since their features correspond to predicates that are not copredicable, that is, predicates that uniquely apply to only animals or only plants. Triffids, then, would cause a violation of the M constraint. Incidentally, if entities like triffids were to appear tomorrow in Times Square, they would not constitute a disproof of the theory. Rather, one would expect people to attempt to force triffids into an M-constrained category. They could do so either by convincing themselves that triffids really were animals that just seemed sort of plantlike or by restructuring their trees so as to change the nature of the plant-animal distinction. Bever and Rosenbaum would probably concur with such a view.

While the predicability tree can constrain the class of possible lexical items in that it disallows all items with component markers that are on different branches, it is nevertheless not a sufficient condition. Take, for example, Goodman's (1965) non-natural predicate "grue," where "grue" "applies to all things examined before time t just in case they are green or to other things just in case they are blue." Note that "examined before t" would not be on a different branch from color predicates; it would simply be above them in the tree. "Grue" is unsatisfactory, as Marshall (1970) points out, because it violates certain "spatio-temporal contiguity constraints" and not because it creates a category mistake.

Similarity

As the ontological tree seems to predict certain intuitions about similarity, it can be related to other psychological research on similarity, specifically to an influential article by Tversky (1977). Tversky proposes "a new set-theoretical approach to similarity . . . in which objects are represented as sets of features, and similarity is described as a feature matching process." Thus similarity is a function of the psychologically natural features that truthfully apply to two things. While the function that determines similarity is fairly intricate, one of its more straightforward aspects is monotonicity.

For any objects a, b, and c, and for sets of features A, B, and C that belong to those objects respectively, Tversky argues that the similarity between a and b is greater than that between a and c whenever $A \cup B \supset A \cup C$, $A - B \subset A - C$, and $B - A \subset C - A$, that is, "whenever those features common to A and B are a superset of those features common to A and C, and whenever those features in A and not in B are a subset of those features in A and not in C, and whenever those features in B and not in A are a subset of those features in C and not in A, then a is more similar to b than to c." Moreover, if two of these conditions are equalities and the third still holds, then a is still more similar to b than to c.

This law can be applied to the ontological tree (Fig. 16). Each ontological category is associated with sets of necessary features where each such set is denoted by a capital letter. Thus the class of physical objects might have such features as "has mass" or "has volume." Classes below physical objects, such as animals, have all the features of physical objects plus additional features, such as "has cellular structure," "grows," or "reproduces."

Given this arrangement of features and the fact that Tversky's theory is meant to apply to similarity between any objects that are delimited by features, including classes, his theory would predict the relative similarities between the class

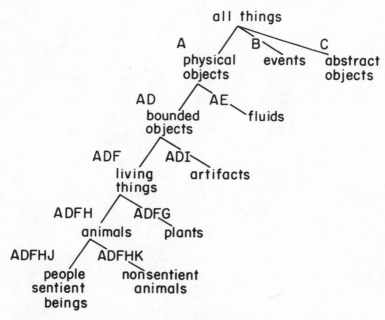

Figure 16. *Tree showing a set-theoretical approach to similarity*

of sentient beings and that of either nonsentient animals or plants (classes I, II, and III, respectively, Fig. 17). The Venn diagram of the three classes shows these class interrelations. The intersection of I and II consists of *HADF*, while the intersection of I and III consists of *ADF*, satisfying the condition $A \cup B \supset A \cup C$, where $A = $ I, $B = $ II, and $C = $ III. The condition $A - B \subset A - C$ is also satisfied, since the features that belong to I and not to II are those in class *J*, while the features that belong to I and not to III are those in classes *J* and *H*. Finally, the tree is indeterminate with respect to the third condition $B - A \subset C - A$, since the features that belong to II and not to I (those in *K*) are not necessarily a subset of the features that belong to III and not I (those in *G*). According to Tversky's theory, if they were equally salient, then the other two conditions would be sufficient to predict that I and II are more similar than I and III. Unfortunately, one cannot be sure that the set of features *G*

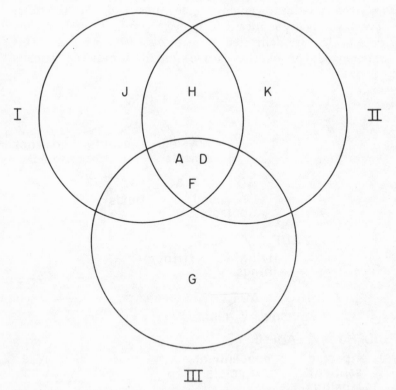

Figure 17.   *Venn diagram showing a set-theoretical approach to similarity*

and *K* would necessarily be equal; at least this cannot be inferred from the predicability theory.

Tversky's theory cannot therefore be applied in its entirety to the ontological tree, since certain cases are indeterminate. Nonetheless, if the two conditions that do apply to the tree are regarded as a special case of Tversky's theory, the predictions derived about the relative similarity judgments are identical to those that follow from the rule that accounts for similarity in terms of the predicability tree. Thus, to the extent that this case is a valid interpretation of Tversky's theory, the similarity relations captured by the tree are in accord with a theoretical model of similarity that has been extremely successful in accounting for the other aspects of similarity.

Many other features of Tversky's work on similarity probably do not apply to the ontological tree. Thus, Tversky is able to model cases where features seem to be organized around central prototypes. Also, certain properties of assymetry are probably not relevant because they are dependent on the notion of prototypes, and prototypes are not likely to be an important factor with ontological categories.

Metaphor

The tree appears to predict, at least in some cases, good metaphors. In general, the prediction will be that those predicates which are only a branch away from a term will make better metaphors with that term than predicates that are further away. For example, it is metaphorically easy to apply plant predicates to animals ("wilted man," "blooming young girl," but not so easy to apply event predicates to animals ("the rabbit happened," "the dog was on Friday," "the man was an hour long").

While there thus seems to be some truth to the tree's prediction, it is unfortunately an oversimplification. Metaphors are extremely complicated, and it is unlikely that any one mechanism is responsible for all of them. One counterexample to the prediction would be the fact that "sterile argument" makes a fine metaphor even though "sterile" is very far from abstract things in the tree. In fact, one of the curious things about metaphor is that virtually any predicate-term combination can, with the proper glossing, become an acceptable metaphor.

One reason the tree may reflect some but not all metaphors could be that metaphor construction involves perception of some sort of similarity between a term or predicate in the metaphor and a term or predicate that could be used literally (cf.

Leech, 1974; Billow, 1977; Tversky, 1977). This does not mean, however, that similarity alone is sufficient to explain all metaphors (Black, 1955). Since the predicability tree does predict similarity ratings of a certain type, it is not surprising that the tree should have some relation to the ease of interpreting metaphors. However, since similarity judgments can also be made on a variety of different dimensions, it also makes sense that many metaphors cannot be predicted from the tree.

Despite these limitations, it is nonetheless remarkable that Levin (1977), in attempting to give an account of how features appear to be transferred to form metaphors, represents the features in a hierarchy that is nearly identical to the ontological tree. Moreover, he argues for its hierarchical nature as opposed to a cross-classification system.

In sum, while the theory of ontological knowledge breaks new ground and addresses issues that have been investigated only indirectly in the past, it also has a surprising number of relations to other research in psychology. In some cases, such as semantic memory research, the relations are more indirect than might at first appear; while in other cases, such as possible lexical items, the relations are straightforward.

In terms of empirical data, the theory of ontological knowledge and the four previous studies were in remarkable accord with most prior work in a variety of areas. In fact, some of that work can be taken as lending support to the theory (e.g. Clark and Begun, 1971; Bever and Rosenbaum, 1971; Tversky, 1977). At a theoretical level, the theory offers a new context within which to view prior research and suggests reinterpretations of past studies. Thus, much of the work on semantic memory and natural categories presupposes, although usually not in an explicit manner, ontological categories and their structural properties.

6 | Origins of Ontological Knowledge

NOW THAT THERE IS a precise and empirically successful way of characterizing one aspect of human knowledge, the structure of ontological categories, which is reflected in a variety of conceptual and linguistic tasks, often via the predicability tree, the origins of that knowledge can be explored. Several developmental questions pertain directly to the theory. Do children have the intuitions that comprise the four phenomena? Are they able to distinguish falsehood from anomaly, natural from nonnatural classes, similarity from dissimilarity, and copredication from incompatibility? Because one underlying aspect of knowledge is supposed to account for all four phenomena, does this mean that if children have intuitions about one phenomenon, they must also have intuitions about the other three?

Given that children do have some or all of these intuitions, what sort of representation best corresponds to these intuitions? Is it an M-constrained tree? Perhaps children have intuitions about all four phenomena but are highly unsystematic and frequently violate the M constraint. Since the M constraint requires a rigid hierarchical form of representation, children who honor it must have at least implicit knowledge of class-inclusion relations. Does this mean that children who fail on traditional classification tasks (Inhelder and Piaget, 1964) will also fail to honor the M constraint? If the M constraint partially fulfills the criterion of explanatory adequacy, it might exist in even the youngest children. Chomsky (1975) and Wexler (1978) suggest that constraints are necessary for the acquisition of complex, structured knowledge. For example, Culicover and Wexler (1978) argue that, if reasonable general learning procedures are assumed, it would not seem possible to learn certain aspects of syntax without a priori constraints that are similar to putative universal constraints on syntax. Moreover, even the most behavioristic of philosophers, such as Quine (1953) and Goodman (1965), argue that, because logically there is an indefinite number of ways of parsing up a conceptual domain, there must be a priori cognitive constraints that sharply limit people's natural ways of construing the world; Quine refers to such constraints as "perceptual and conceptual quality spaces." Without such constraints, acquisition and communication of knowledge would be impossible. Quine and Goodman are considered behaviorists because they want to posit the fewest and most general constraints possible.

Does the M constraint serve such a role in the acquisition of ontological knowledge? Is it a built-in constraint that is necessary because it limits the possible ways of conceptualizing the world? If there are children who honor the M constraint, how do the trees representing their intuitions differ from those for adults? Are the immature trees completely different, or is there some systematic way in which they differ? The trees representing children's intuitions might be expected to be less refined than those for adults; that is, they might make fewer categorical distinctions. If so, what are their primitive categories like? Because the tree representation is hierarchical, questions about highly specific patterns of development can be examined, such as how branches are added, what sorts of categorical distinctions are missed, and whether the developmental histories of predicates and terms are different.

Finally, what do the results gathered in answer to these questions tell about children's concepts more generally? What sorts of cognitive structures are required for children to have the four intuitions? How does the M constraint relate to other skills such as classification? Perhaps most important, since the tree is also meant to represent conceptual categorization, what do developing tree structures tell about how children conceive of the world?

To answer these questions, it was necessary to devise a technique that obtained intuitions, if any, from young children and to use those intuitions to construct trees. It is theoretically possible to reconstruct a tree using intuitions about any of the four phenomena, but in four developmental studies intuitions about only the first phenomenon, anomaly, were used. One of the more important reasons for doing so was that the first phenomenon lent itself to an experimental design that was particularly easy to use with young children.

Children's Intuitions of Anomaly

In general, constructing a tree representation from anomaly intuitions is a two-step process. First, intuitions are obtained about whether each sentence in a set is anomalous or sensible, and a structure is generated out of those intuitions. Should such a structure violate the M constraint, the subject is then questioned to determine if the convergent nodes harbor ambiguities.

In the study of adults, this task was a relatively simple one, as it was easy to convey to adults the notion of anomaly versus falsehood. Moreover, they usually remarked spontaneously on any ambiguities. Children, however, are a different story.

It is possible to train at least some five-year-olds to make judgments about anomaly in contrast to falsehood, but the job takes considerable time. One possible technique is to ask children to tell the experimenter if any of the things the experimenter says "could happen" or "sound O.K." The experimenter may then give a sentence such as "The cow was green." Most children will declare initially that it sounds bad. The experimenter asks why, and the children might respond, "Because they are brown or white." The experimenter might then ask, "But what if you painted the cow green?" The children usually then agree that the sentence is O.K. Next the experimenter gives the children a sentence such as "The idea is red" and, to a "sounds bad" response, may ask, "But what if you painted it red?" Depending on the children's particular intuitions, they might exclaim, "But you can't paint ideas!" In this way, the difference between falsehood and anomaly is conveyed, although it often takes several examples.

The difficulty is that such a training procedure takes a long time and the children have to be frequently reminded of the distinction. The studies of anomaly intuitions therefore used a different method, requiring virtually no training of the children as informants. This technique is based on the fact that a category mistake does not have a truth value, which means that both it and its negation are seen as nonsense. By contrast, the negation of a false sentence must be true. While children may claim that a false sentence and a category mistake are both nonsense, they nonetheless distinguish the two when they are negated. Thus children might say that "The cow was green" and "The idea was green" are both "silly," but they should also claim that "The cow was not green" is O.K., while "The idea was not green" is still "silly." Whether children are basing their judgments on falsehood or anomaly, it is therefore possible to separate anomalous sentences from false ones by presenting, along with every sentence, its negation.

This solution raises a new problem. Young children, and apparently some adults, are not particularly adept with negatives, often misconstruing the scope of the negation operator. Thus, "The idea was not wrinkled" might be interpreted as "It is not possible for the idea to be wrinkled" rather than "The idea was not wrinkled because it was smooth."

To solve this problem, one can use predicate pairs that are implicit negatives of each other, such as polar opposites or antonymous *n*-tuples. Thus, instead of the pair "The idea was wrinkled" and "The idea was not wrinkled," one can use "The idea was wrinkled" and "The idea was smooth." In the case of antonymous *n*-tuples, instead of "The idea was red" and "The idea was not red," one can use "The idea was red" and "The idea was green," "The idea was yellow," "The idea was blue," or "The idea was some other color." It is possible that some of the young children might see some antonyms as synonyms (cf. Clark, 1973). To check for this, a pilot study was conducted in which eight out of ten first-graders were required to have a rough idea of what each member of the predicate pair meant before that pair was used in the study. The actual experimental design also checked for understanding by asking the children to justify all their judgments.

In addition to obtaining intuitions that separate anomalous sentences from those with truth values, one must also find out what terms and predicates, if any, are considered ambiguous. It would be too tedious to ask if every term or predicate is ambiguous. Instead, another technique was employed. The judgments of all possible predicate-term combinations were recorded in such a way that any intersections were immediately apparent after the last sentence had been judged. Suppose, for example, that "is short" spans terms that intersect with those spanned by "is heavy" and "happened yesterday," as follows:

Terms spanned	Predicate	Term
1, 3	is short	1. the recess
1, 2	happened yesterday	2. the collision
3, 4	is heavy	3. the chair
		4. the water

These intersections can be caused by an ambiguity in "the recess" or in "is short" or in both "happened yesterday" and "is heavy." When intersections such as these appeared, the child was asked, "Does 'recess' mean the same thing [is it being used the same way] in 'The recess was short' and 'The recess happened yesterday'?" The child was also asked, "Does 'short' mean the same thing in 'The recess was short' and 'The chair was short'?" In this way, the word that was ambiguous for most adults as well as one control that was a logically possible ambiguity were given to the child.

It may seem unlikely that young children could make judgments about ambiguity. In fact, under the right conditions, it is quite easy for them to do so. While children under six are often poor at picking out an ambiguous term, they are adept at recognizing it if it is shown in different contexts (cf. Keil, in press). For this reason, the task was not above any child's level of ability.

The First Grade-School Study

Sixteen children at each of three grades—Kindergarten, second, and fourth—participated in the first developmental study. In addition, eight sixth-graders participated. The mean ages were 5 years 7 months, 7 years 5 months, 9 years 6 months, and 11 years 5 months, respectively. There were equal numbers of girls and boys in each age group.

The stimuli consisted of two groups of sentences. Both groups contained the same predicates but had different sets of terms (Fig. 18). The purpose of using two different sets of terms was to check on the generality of the results. If nearly identical patterns of results were obtained using different sets of terms, it would be difficult to argue that idiosyncratic predicate-term relations were influencing the results. Ideally, both sets of terms should have been used with each subject, but that would have created too many sentences to give to a child.

Each group of sentences consisted of fourteen predicate pairs in every possible combination with one of the two sets of seven terms. Each predicate pair consisted of opposites (tall-short, alive-dead). It might seem that there would therefore be 196 sentences per child, but actually the number usually was considerably smaller, for the reason that there were two predicate pairs at each node, and these were always presented in the same order (pair 1, then pair 2), though not in immediate succession. In other words, for each node there were four predicates spaced apart in the stimulus set. The order within a pair was randomized for each subject. If a child stated that a particular predicate-term combination was "O.K.," there was no need to

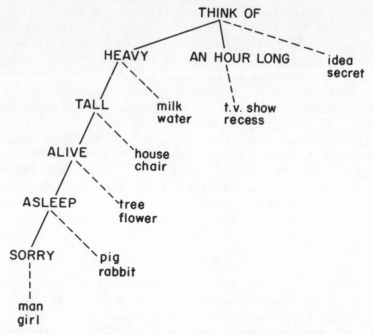

Figure 18. *Predicability tree used in first grade-school study*

proceed with the remaining three predicates because any judgment of sensibleness meant that the relevant node existed. If,
however, the child's answer of "O.K." was different from the
adult pattern, then the remaining predicates were used. For any
answers of "silly," additional predicates were used until either
an "O.K." judgment was given or all four had been used. On
the average, each child received about 125 sentences.

It might be argued that this procedure biased the data, but it
could have done so only in the direction of minimizing developmental effects. That is, any time a developmental difference
occurred, it was doubled-checked. Any sensibleness judgments
in accordance with adult intuitions were not checked. Thus
the developmental results may be underrepresented, but if
strong developmental results survived this procedure, then
there is reason to be confident in them. It is also true that this
procedure reduced somewhat the chances of an M violation appearing since some developmental differences could cause the
appearance of an M. But this was not a problem because there
were still many possible occasions for the M constraint to be
violated.

The sentences were presented in random order with one exception: all terms that went with a given predicate were presented successively, though in random order. Pilot work had indicated that the session would proceed more quickly as both children and adults were able to "tune in" to the concept behind the predicate and quickly evaluate successive terms.

Predicates were always spaced apart from their opposites. The reason was that giving a predicate right after its opposite had caused some children in a pilot study automatically to change their judgments from "silly" to "O.K." without really thinking. Most children were not even aware that both poles of an opposite pair had been presented. In the case of antonymous *n*-tuples, the second presentation included several members of the *n*-tuple in succession.

After each child's answer, he or she was asked, "How could an *x* be *P*?" to justify answers of "O.K." and "Why can't an *x* be *P*?" to justify answers of "silly." If these justifications indicated that the child had misunderstood a predicate, or if the child said "I don't know," the additional predicates were used.

In addition, for any answer differing from the adult model and for an equal number of control answers, the children were pressed to make sure they were not using ellipses. For example, if a child said that "An idea is an hour long," the experimenter asked, "Was it the idea that was an hour long or just the thinking of the idea?" A control for this might be, "Was it the recess that was an hour long, or just the playing of the recess?" If the child answered something like, "No, it's just the thinking that's an hour long," he or she was then asked, "Are you sure?" and was given the initial predicate-term pair again and asked for a second judgment. This second judgment was taken as the final one.

The probe questions served four purposes. First, if more than 25 percent of any child's answers were "I don't know" or if the child seemed to have no understanding of more than 25 percent of the word meanings, the child was dropped from the study. Second, on several occasions, the probe questions served to make the child change an impulsively generated response to a more reflective one. After asking "Are you sure?" the experimenter recorded the later response. Third, the probe questions often revealed blatant ambiguities, which were nevertheless tested for at the end of the session, and they served as a check for ellipsis. And fourth, the probe questions gave the experimenter a feeling for what was actually happening with the children. For example, in answering the questions, the children often gave an indication of whether they were interpreting various words metaphorically.

The importance of the probe questions should not be underestimated. Several children did change their answers after a probe. Also, upon seeing that there was a series of probes for all sentences, the children realized that they would have to give answers that they could justify. This virtually did away with problems such as perseveration; nevertheless, a few control items were included to check for this contingency.

All "don't know" answers to probe questions were recorded, as well as all answers suggesting ambiguities. All responses indicating lack of understanding of a word were also recorded. In addition, answers to probe questions were written down verbatim whenever possible.

Each experimental session began by giving the child two examples each of anomalous and sensible sentences: "The door ran across the room," "The door was brown," "The rock was big," and "The rock was angry." All children were also given practice probes. No feedback was given as to the correctness of their answers. The instructions to the children stressed that they were to judge a sentence as "O.K." if it "could happen" or "if you think of it as being O.K. somewhere." The intent was to bias the children toward judging on the basis of sense.

The practice sentences may have somewhat biased the children's responses in that, even though no feedback was given, the situation implied that probably one of each pair was incorrect. However, the position of the incorrect one was switched in the two pairs. If a child was completely unable to give a judgment, he or she was dropped from the study.

After the practice items, the children received the test sentences. If a child paused after presentation of any test sentence, the experimenter followed up with "Could an x be P?" This also helped the child to think in terms of possibility.

Embedded randomly within the test sentences were two control sentences that were used as a test against perseveration. One sentence was blatantly true to the child, the other blatantly anomalous. The true sentence was "The little boy/girl was x years old," where the sentential subject matched the child's sex and x matched the child's stated age. The anomalous sentence was a minor variant of one of the two example sentences—the one that the child got right. Instead of "The door ran across the room," the child was given "The door walked upstairs"; and instead of "The rock was angry," the child was given "The stick was angry." If a child missed any of these, he or she was dropped from the study.

After completion of all predicate-term judgments, there was a short conversation period during which the experimenter checked the data sheet for ambiguities. If there were any intersections of term classes, the experimenter gave the child three practice examples of obvious ambiguities in different contexts ("bat," "glasses," "son/sun"). The child was then given the actual predicate or term in the two contexts. These test items were embedded among several controls consisting of other predicates and terms that had been used in the study.

Tree Representations

From each child's responses a tree or partial lattice was constructed, depending on whether the M constraint was honored (Figs. A1–A56 in Appendix C). There were no significant differences between the trees constructed with one set of terms versus the other. For this reason, the two groups of trees were pooled. There were also no sex differences. The results of this and other developmental studies are occasionally described in terms of "a child's tree" or a child's "having a tree," not in the literal sense since the tree is actually a characterization of a child's knowledge rather than the knowledge itself, but simply for ease of exposition.

Violations of the M constraint were extremely rare. In fact, out of at least 100,000 possible occasions for violation, only six cases were seen, and three of these were equivocal in that the children were not at all sure what a particular term or predicate meant; that is, they vacillated between an M-constrained interpretation and one that created a violation. All six cases involved predicates and terms pertaining to events and abstract objects.

Eight apparent M violations were resolved as ambiguities. Most of these involved "is short," meaning short in duration or length, and "is heavy," meaning "having mass" or "profound." This low number would have provided strong evidence that children tend to honor the M constraint even if the ambiguity test had not been used.

The conclusion is that, at least for the predicates and terms used in the study, the M constraint is honored scrupulously by children as young as five years. There is still the very real question of whether they would honor the M constraint for any predicates and terms. The terms and predicates used in this study were not selected at random; rather they were picked as ones that best captured the experimenter's intuitions and that young children were likely to understand. Three sample trees generated by a five-, seven-, and nine-year-old, along with a sampling of their answers to probe questions, give an informal idea of how the trees develop. More reliable developmental patterns, can then be derived from the data as a whole. Incidentally, whenever an asterisk appears next to a predicate, it means that the predicate is a backup predicate. Such predicates were used whenever the child did not understand the first predicate (one of those shown in Fig. 18).

The tree generated by a five-year-old's intuitions was one of the two or three more primitive trees (Fig. 19; see also Figs. A2 and A3 in Appendix C). Only two groups of terms appear to be distinguished by this tree: those terms that denote living objects and those that denote all other things.

This five-year-old child did not differentiate ideas and recesses from physical object terms. An idea or a recess was just as able to be heavy or tall as was a chair. Not surprisingly, this child also moved the event-specific predicate ("was an hour long") up the tree to the top node, thus eliminating the class of events as a separate entity. Consequently, all things could be an hour long.

It would have been surprising if the child had said that "was an hour long" applied just to recesses and yet at the same time let recesses be heavy. If children are being consistent in their ontological classification of things, they should either have recesses spanned only by "was an hour long" or move "was an hour long" up the tree. This consistency in conceptual categorization is equivalent to honoring the M constraint.

Figure 19. *Predicability tree showing a five-year-old's intuitions*

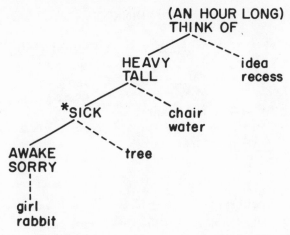

Figure 20. *Predicability tree showing a seven-year-old's intuitions*

The answers to the probe questions indicate that this five-year-old was sincere in his beliefs about the physical properties of what adults consider events and abstract objects. For example, when he was asked how a recess could be heavy, he replied "'cause it's all outside and that's very heavy." When asked if the recess itself or just all outside was heavy, the child responded, "It is the recess since it is outside." These answers demonstrate that the responses were not disguised ellipses or playful responses. The child also stated that ideas were very light, which argues against the claim that the child was merely having problems with a specific lexical item ("heavy").

In the tree representation of a seven-year-old's intuitions, the child is beginning to make more distinctions and now seems to have four categories: animals, plants, nonliving physical things, and nonphysical things (Fig. 20). The tree illustrates one fairly common pattern among the five- and seven-year-olds, that while they seemed to be aware that the terms denoting nonphysical things were different from other terms, they often did not yet have any predicates for nonphysical things. For this reason, "was an hour long" was said to apply sensibly to all terms. In many cases these children did not have any clear idea of the meaning of "was an hour long," which is indicated in the figures by being put in parentheses, where parentheses signify a large number of "I don't know" answers to probe questions about that predicate.

In the representation of a nine-year-old's intuitions, the only distinctions not present at this point were those between

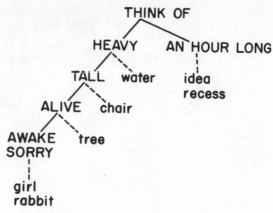

Figure 21. *Predicability tree showing a nine-year-old's intuitions*

humans and other mammals and between events and abstract objects (Fig. 21). At this stage, the predicate "was an hour long" has become specific for nonphysical objects. This child said that an idea was an hour long "because that's how long it took to think it." The child did not back down when asked if it was the idea itself or the thinking of the idea that was an hour long. He said that it was both. These two collapses—events with abstract objects and humans with other animals—were almost always the last to give way to the type of structure seen in the adult.

Increasing Differentiation

The data can be analyzed from three different viewpoints, each of which provides different insights into what develops. First is the degree of differentiation. The mean number of term categories represented in the trees for each age group provide evidence that the trees become more complex with increasing age. There was a regular pattern of increase from 3.9 categories in kindergartners to 4.6 categories in the second grade, 5.4 categories in the fourth grade, and 6.2 categories in the sixth grade. These increases with age were significant both as a group (analysis of variance, $p < .01$) and individually (Scheffé test, $p < .05$).

Perhaps the single most important developmental finding is that the trees appear to develop in a characteristic manner. Thus, immature trees differed from adult trees in a systematic fashion. A collapsed version of the adult tree almost invariably consisted of certain predicates being higher up in the tree than

Table 9 *Children's trees that were perfect collapses of adult model*

Grade	Perfect Collapse	One Inversion	Two Inversions
K (n = 16)	63%	31%	6%
2 (n = 16)	94%	6%	0%
4 (n = 16)	100%	0%	0%
6 (n = 8)	100%	0%	0%

in adults; it was rarely the case that a collapsed tree was due to a predicate being lower in the tree. It was also extremely rare for two predicates to be in an inverse dominance relation to each other in an immature tree ("is alive" spanning more terms than "is tall"). In fact, this happened only seven out of a possible 1008 times.

The point is that trees seem to obey rigid developmental constraints. Development appears to consist of restricting the scope of predicates to narrower and narrower classes of terms. There are certainly other ways in which immature trees could differ from mature ones, such as that predicates could be overly restrictive; but, they were not seen here. The percentage of children at each age whose trees were perfect collapses of the adult model was quite high (Table 9, Fig. 18). That is, to generate a child's tree from the adult model, all that is required is to move predicates together along the solid spanning lines and not hop over any. It is as if the predicates were beads on a string. Even among the kindergartners, 63 percent of all trees were perfect collapses, 31 percent required only one switch in a dominance relation to be perfect, and 6 percent required switches in two dominance relations. In the second, fourth, and sixth grades, virtually all trees were perfect collapses. Interpreted at a deeper level, these findings suggest both that the child's ontological knowledge develops by making more and more refined distinctions, and that it is these distinctions which allow the child to use predicates in an increasingly restrictive fashion.

Ordered and Asymmetrical Differentiation

The data can also be analyzed from the viewpoint of the percentages of children in each age group whose intuitions resulted in a particular collapse (Table 10). The term collapse between events and abstract objects can also be included here because there was no unique predicate for abstract things and

Table 10   *Collapses of adjacent predicates and term categories for events and abstract objects in first grade-school study*

Collapse	Grade			
	K	2	4	6
SORRY/AWAKE	44%	44%	81%	25%
AWAKE/ALIVE	50%	25%	0%	0%
ALIVE/TALL	0%	0%	0%	0%
TALL/HEAVY	63%	44%	25%	0%
HEAVY/THINK OF	50%	13%	0%	0%
THINK OF/AN HOUR LONG	44%	38%	0%	0%
events/abstract objects	81%	75%	56%	50%

therefore the term collapse was the only index of a category collapse in that area of the tree.

The developmental finding of decreasing numbers of collapses with increasing age was well distributed throughout the tree. Five of the seven tabulated collapses showed this pattern, which is evidence for the generality of the finding. It demonstrates that the tree as a whole develops and not just one or two nodes.

The two cases where collapse did not monotonically decrease with age were those between "awake" and "sorry" and between "alive" and "tall." In the case of "awake" and "sorry," there actually seemed to be an increase in the incidence of collapses from the second to fourth grades followed by a sharp decrease in the sixth grade. Answers by the children to the probe questions suggest that an ambiguity in the word "sorry" was the reason for this pattern. The younger children often thought that people are sorry only when they say they are sorry. This interpretation of "sorry" marks a clear distinction between humans and other animals since only humans talk. For this reason, it is not surprising that several of the youngest children were able to distinguish "sorry" from "awake." On the contrary, the older children—fourth and sixth graders—seemed to be using the adult sense of "sorry" in which one has only to feel sorry to be legitimately sorry. Even some adults have difficulty deciding whether this version of "sorry" can be sensibly applied to animals. It is unfortunate that this double sense of "sorry" was a factor, as it makes the developmental changes appear less dramatic than they are.

In the case of "alive" and "tall," there was no developmental trend because no children at any age had intuitions that re-sulted in a collapse of those two predicates. Apparently, this is by far the strongest distinction to be made in the tree.

Distinctions were made in a certain order; that is, some col-lapses disappeared earlier than others. The order included roughly five steps: alive vs. tall, heavy vs. think of, awake vs. alive and think of vs. an hour long, heavy vs. tall, and event terms vs. abstract object terms and sorry vs. awake. In this re-spect the predicates differentiated in an ordered fashion. The differentiation was also "asymmetrical" in that, when a dis-tinction was first made between two predicates that formerly shared the same node, it was not always the case that both predicates would then each span just their "adult-appropriate" term classes. Rather, one predicate often seemed to be much clearer in the child's mind and would "move down" to its ap-propriate term class first, while the other predicate continued to stay at the upper node with the child often unsure about its meaning.

For example, several of the younger children had trees with "heavy," "think of," and "an hour long" all at the top node, often with other predicates. The first development with this three-predicate cluster was normally for "heavy" to move down the tree and span only terms that denote physical ob-jects. At this stage "an hour long" was usually still at the top node along with "think of." This arrangement would seem to suggest that there was a point in development where children thought that physical objects could have temporal duration but did not think that nonphysical objects could be heavy. This, however, is probably not the best interpretation. The younger children's responses suggested that they had a murky idea of what "an hour long" meant. While they often said that it could sensibly apply to all terms, they were not at all confident in that judgment, as evidenced by frequent vacillations and nu-merous "don't know" answers to probe questions.

This difficulty with "an hour long," as well as with other predicates and terms, can be understood more clearly by a rein-terpretation in terms of the development of ontological knowl-edge. That is, if the use of a certain predicate such as "tall" sug-gests that all terms spanned by "tall" are conceived of as types of physical objects, then the ontological categories would ap-pear to differentiate at five levels corresponding to the predi-cate collapses: living things vs. other physical objects, physical objects vs. all other things, plants vs. animals and events vs. physical objects, physical objects with boundaries vs. physical objects without boundaries, and events vs. abstract objects and humans vs. animals.

Implicit in this ordering is the assumption that the asymmetry between predicates such as "heavy" and "an hour long" is an indication of the developmental primacy of the category demarcated by the predicate that differentiates first ("heavy"). Even though "an hour long" might remain at the top node of the tree, this does not mean that all things are conceived of as events. Rather, it appears from the answers to probe questions that the children developed through a precise sequence with regard to the predicate "an hour long."

The very youngest children seemed to think that all things were physical objects, and they therefore had a roughly appropriate meaning for "heavy" but did not have much of an idea of what "an hour long" meant. In the few cases where they did have a rough idea of "an hour long," they put it on a branch below "heavy," as if events and abstract objects were a distinguishable subclass of physical objects (Figs. A5, A6, A8, A16, A28 in Appendix C). This kind of restructuring of the tree is evidence of their conviction that everything was physical.

Slightly older children were aware that there were things that were nonphysical, but they knew little more about them than that. As a result, they did think that "heavy" was no longer appropriate for events and abstract objects, but they still were not clear as to what "an hour long" meant.

Still older children realized that "an hour long" applied only to nonphysical things. Probe answers indicated that they knew considerably more, that "an hour long" applied to things that were events. Their only problem was that they did not seem to realize that there were other nonphysical things besides events; and for this reason, ideas and secrets were understood as types of events.

Finally, the oldest children made the distinction between events and abstract objects. However, this last distinction is sufficiently subtle that even some adults failed to make it.

In this progression categories often seem to develop out of other categories. That is, children do not suddenly realize that there are physical objects, events, and abstract objects; rather, they suddenly realize that some things are not physical objects. They are not sure what these are; they just know what they are not. Moreover, younger children do not start with a syncretic concept of "physical object-abstract object-event" out of which the three separate notions emerge. Rather, they have only the concept "physical object," and everything is considered to be a physical object. When children first make the distinction, they do not have an equally clear idea of what both categories are like; on the contrary, they only know that there are some unclear things that do not fit into the clear class of physical objects.

The same pattern is seen at other nodes. The class of abstract things seems to differentiate out of the class of events, the class of liquids out of the class of objects with boundaries, and the class of plants out of the class of animals.

In sum, the asymmetric development of predicates out of a cluster and the high level of uncertainty with the predicate left behind suggest a much more important developmental phenomenon at the ontological level, namely that categories appear to develop out of other categories. This conclusion is supported by the types of answers children gave to probe questions. However, all categories do not necessarily develop out of others. There might be cases where categories develop out of a syncretic complex, even though this is unlikely if one accepts a parsimonious theory of conceptual development.

Furthermore, because the data consist of intuitions about predicates and terms and the conclusions about ontological knowledge are inferences made on the basis of a variety of suggestive facts, some or all of these phenomena could be exclusively problems with word meanings, and the underlying ontological knowledge could already be in the adult form. However, the possibility that all these phenomena are simply a consequence of an isolated semantic system is extremely unlikely. For example, there is no good reason that both sets of terms used in the study should show precisely the same patterns. This is not to say that children's meanings for these terms and predicates do not change dramatically with development. Instead, these changes do not occur simply in isolation but are strongly driven by underlying ontological development. There may well be other semantic changes not related to ontological development, but it would certainly appear that ontological knowledge plays an important role.

Terms Denoting Classes before Predicates

One other result that appeared to occur frequently in the study was for immature trees to have a term class that had no unique predicates. In such cases, the predicate that uniquely spanned the same class of terms for adults usually was at a higher node in the child's tree. A good example of this pattern appears in the seven-year-old's tree.

The pattern seems to be that children become aware of a category via its terms before they become aware of its unique predicates. The small tree used in the study only begins to give an answer to the question of how general the pattern is. With only seven branches, it does not show clearly what distinctions are being made. For example, if children were to learn the terms denoting events before they learned the predicates, they would say that "was an hour long" is predicable of all terms, while recesses can be spanned only by "is thought about" and "was an hour long." If, however, they were to learn predicates before terms, they would let recesses and vacations be spanned by various physical object predicates and the predicate "was an hour long" would not span anything. Unfortunately, this second pattern of results would not necessarily represent the learning of intensions before extensions in that one could not be sure what the predicate "was an hour long" meant to the children. Since it would not span anything, it could be just nonsense to them. If, however, the children could give various appropriate synonyms, the predicate must have a meaning for them. In addition, one could not be sure where to put such a predicate in the tree since it could be on any branch from top to bottom.

With these cautions in mind, the data nevertheless suggest powerfully that categories are first represented by terms. In all fifty-four trees generated in the development study, there were no cases where a predicate spanned no terms; however, there were several instances where classes of terms had no unique predicates.

In brief, two conclusions may be drawn from the developmental data in the first grade-school study. First, the M constraint is honored at all ages. Second, the trees illustrate a specific developmental pattern, namely increasing differentiation and hierarchical organization. In addition, there were two tentative findings: new categories seem to be distinguished first by sets of terms and only later by sets of predicates, and certain patterns of predicate and term differentiation suggest that new categories often seem to develop out of old ones rather than out of hybrids.

Methodological Issues

Two methodological issues raise the question of whether the results could be due to other factors not central to the proposed theory. One objection that might be raised against the methodology of the developmental study is that it is not really measuring conceptual developmental or even semantic development; rather, it is simply showing that young children are much more willing to make metaphors than adults are. The results could thus be a consequence of metaphorical extension. It may be that children can honor all the adult distinctions if they have a mind to do so.

The literature on the development of metaphors (e.g. Gardner et al., 1975) is not particularly helpful in this context. While Gardner shows that young children seem to be able to produce and understand metaphors, it is not at all apparent that they think that all such metaphors are really metaphorical and not literal. This issue has not been addressed sufficiently in the literature. As there is no contradictory evidence, many of the so-called metaphors in children's speech would appear to be their literal beliefs. This is not to deny that other metaphors may be seen by them as such. In fact, one distinct possibility is that those adult metaphors that violated even the children's trees would be seen as metaphors, while those that did not would be interpreted literally.

This proposal in itself is unlikely to prove that the developmental data do not simply represent creative play with the language. A more compelling reason derives from the data themselves. The judgments of the children all conformed to very regular patterns that almost always honored the M constraint. If the children were just being playful with the language, it is unlikely that their deviations from the adults would have formed such orderly patterns. If an adult were to decide to be more "creative and playful" and use many metaphors, he would not just move predicates higher up in the tree as the children did; he would also be likely to violate the M constraint.

The possibility that the tree is measuring the child's knowledge of empirical truths is the other methodological issue, as it was in the adult studies. The argument is that the trees might not represent predicability or conceptual categories but rather might depict what facts the child has learned about the world. Perhaps the child is responding on the basis of validity and not conceivability. The results could thus be merely a reflection of judgments of empirical plausibility.

Several pieces of evidence work against such an interpretation. First, the pilot work indicated that very young children can distinguish anomalous from false sentences. Gleitman et al. (1974) report a similar finding where an admittedly precocious seven-year-old was able to distinguish "The color green frightens George," which she considered false, from "George frightens the color green," which she said "sounds okay, but it's stupid, it's stupid."

More direct evidence that the children in this study were not just making judgments of plausibility appears in the pattern of their responses to predicate-term pairs that described implausible situations. Since the children were not explicitly trained to respond in terms of possibility, any responses indicating the acceptability of implausible sentences represent spontaneous recognition of the fact that implausible sentences are different from anomalous ones. A sizable percentage of the children at each age said that the implausible sentences "The flower is heavy," "The pig is tall," and "The rabbit is tall" were acceptable (Table 11).

Perhaps the best evidence against the argument that the developmental data represent just the child's knowledge of the world and not differences in conceptual or semantic representations appears in the children's deviations from the adult pattern. A large number of children said that recesses could be heavy and that secrets could be tall in the spatial sense. It is very difficult to imagine that they ever could have experienced true instances of these sentences and yet also have the same semantic representations for these sentences as adults.

This methodological issue is related to the more general question of what sorts of linguistic intuitions the young child is able to use. The claim is not made that the young child has all the intuitions of an adult or even any of them at the adult's level of sophistication. Rather, the argument is that five-year-olds, and probably younger children, are capable of giving judgments about anomaly that are distinct from those about falsehood. It is quite another matter to ask at what level they are aware of this distinction.

Not much is known about the nature and development of

Table 11   *Implausible statements judged to be sensible*

	Grade			
Implausible	K (n = 8)	2 (n = 8)	4 (n = 8)	6 (n = 4)
The Flower Is Heavy	38%	38%	13%	50%
The Pig Is Tall	63%	38%	25%	50%
The Rabbit Is Tall	63%	38%	50%	75%

the child's linguistic intuitions. The pioneering work done by Gleitman et al. (1974) has shown that young children are considerably more sophisticated than was previously believed. There are still many unanswered questions, however. Beyond the question of when various intuitions emerge, there are the much more difficult questions of why intuitions emerge when they do, how they develop, and what they tell about the underlying competence of the child. There is also the question of the extent to which metalinguistic awareness lags behind competence in a particular area. Perhaps children are capable of honoring all the adult predicability relations at a much earlier age than that at which they can first provide intuitions. This is highly unlikely, however, because if it were true, once the child gained such an awareness, his or her judgments should rapidly come to mirror those of the adult. It is hard to imagine how the "meta-ability" itself could systematically alter the trees so as to create the developmental patterns observed.

Limitations and Unanswered Questions

While the study has uncovered several interesting developmental phenomena, other questions remain unanswered. First, would the same developmental patterns be seen for other nodes, for different predicates and terms at the same nodes, and for different tree configurations? It is possible that the nodes and lexical items selected in the study have certain idiosyncratic properties that are not representative of the predicability tree as a whole. Perhaps other nodes or lexical items would yield M-constraint violations in children, or even if the M-constraint were honored, the various types of collapses might not be nearly as systematic or rule-governed. Similarly, a different tree configuration with more left-right branching and less top-bottom branching might have different developmental properties. In sum, the generality of the findings reported in the study is not known.

Second, precisely what aspects of the children's knowledge are responsible for the collapsed trees? There is still some uncertainty as to whether the children's collapsed trees are solely consequences of differences in conceptual knowledge or whether in some cases collapses are simply a consequence of children having a different meaning for certain words. While the evidence from the study certainly points to a conceptual basis for most of the collapses, there are still questions about the role of word meanings. A more extensive chain of probe questions could help to resolve these questions.

Third, how does a child go from a smaller tree to a larger tree? The study provided several "snapshots" of trees at different stages of development, and these "snapshots" suggested a highly systematic way in which trees develop. But it is still not known what goes on in children's heads when they change tree structures. Is it a virtually instantaneous process, or do they seem to have both representations for a time and oscillate between them? Do they become uncertain during such transitions, or are they convinced of their beliefs? Again, a more extensive set of probe questions may shed some light on these questions.

Fourth, the study suggests that children as young as five honor the M constraint. Is that also the case for younger children? Is it even possible to elicit intuitions from preschoolers that will permit the construction of trees for them? If such trees can be constructed, will they still have branches or will they be collapsed to one node?

Fifth, are the developmental patterns closely linked to English, or are they more independent of specific languages? If ontological development is the driving force behind the tree, the latter case would be more correct, but not necessarily so, since a specific language may influence the structure of ontological knowledge.

In summary, it is possible to use children's intuitions about at least one of the four phenomena, anomaly, to generate tree representations of their ontological knowledge. The results suggest that children as young as five honor the M constraint, even though their trees differ from adult ones by having many fewer nodes. The trees developed according to specific patterns that suggested certain views of conceptual development.

7 | Follow-up Studies

ERTAIN QUESTIONS WERE RAISED by the first study of anomaly intuitions in grade-school children. How general are the developmental patterns? What aspects of the children's knowledge are responsible for their having different tree representations? How does the child make the transition from a smaller to a larger tree? Are systematic tree structures seen in even younger children? Do the same developmental phenomena hold across languages?

A second, more extensive grade-school study was conducted to answer the first three questions and a more informal preschool study was conducted to begin to answer the fourth question. Finally, a study in Puerto Rico addressed the last question.

The Second Grade-School Study

In an attempt to answer the first three questions, a study was conducted using a new tree structure (Fig. 22). One of the new nodes represents machines or artifacts with a functional purpose, that is, physical objects constructed by man for a functional purpose. This seems to be a basic distinction for adults, and it is of interest to know when children make such a distinction.

Another new node represents intentional events, that is, events on which a moral evaluation can be placed because they are caused by an individual. These events contrasted with naturally occurring events where no sentient being is responsible for their occurrence. No term, except possibly "natural event," must necessarily be put at the node corresponding to natural events, because depending on one's scientific or religious beliefs, events such as thunderstorms and sunrises can be consid-

85

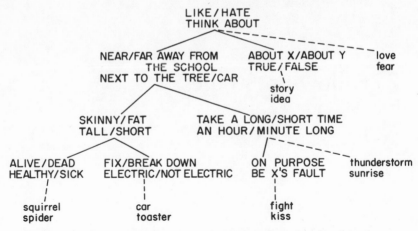

Figure 22. *Predicability tree used in second grade-school study*

ered intentional events. The crucial distinction between intentional and natural events is that, in cases where one accepts that event x is a natural event, one realizes that it cannot be evaluated morally. It is of interest to know how children learn the distinction between intentional and natural events since the recognition of intention has been claimed to be a crucial process in theories of moral development (e.g. Piaget, 1932).

Still another node represents things that have spatial locations and is designated by the predicates "near" and "next to." This node covers both events and physical objects. Since some children appear to treat events as physical objects, it is of interest to see how they interpret predicates that span both.

Finally, the terms "love" and "fear" represent a category corresponding to states of affairs, in this case human states of affairs. It is of interest to see if children treat these abstract objects as they treat abstract objects that correspond to propositional information.

All other nodes were the same as those used in the first grade-school study (Fig. 18). Different predicates and terms were used, however, to check that the results of the first study were not simply a consequence of the particular predicates and terms that were used there. Also, a wider variety of syntactic predicate-term combinations were used, varying from term-copula-adjective to subject-predicate-term to term-adjective-prepositional phrase. Again this helped to test the generality of the results. Because the pilot vocabulary testing with first-graders sharply limited the predicates and terms that were usable, a few predicates were repeated from the first study. Certain categories were also omitted from the new tree in order to keep the total number of predicate-term combinations at a reasonable level. Nodes representing sentient beings, plants and fluids were omitted.

The general configurational properties of the new tree differ from those of the simplified experimental tree (Fig. 18). It was felt that these configurational changes would provide a more strenuous test of the developmental phenomena uncovered by the first grade-school study. The main configurational difference is that the new tree has more left-right branching and less top-down branching. Thus, the longest sequence of top-down predicate-predicate links is three links ("like"–"alive"), as opposed to five links earlier ("think"–"girl"). A second difference between the two trees is that the new one has more cases in which both branches below a superordinate node have unique predicates: there was one such case before ("heavy" and "an hour long") and are three such cases in the second tree ("alive" and "fix," "skinny" and "a long time," and "near" and "about x").

These differences in general tree structure provide more extensive tests of the findings of the first study for a number of reasons. First, the increase in cases where both immediately subordinate branches have unique predicates results in a more rigorous test of the M constraint since, with predicates at both nodes, there are more chances of an M constraint being violated.

Second, the pattern of increasing differentiation is tested more carefully since, instead of having just two collapse routes as there were before ("alive" → "think about" and "an hour long" → "think about"), the tree now has four such routes ("alive" → "like," "fix" → "like," "on purpose" → "like," and "about x" → "like"). A collapse route is defined as a top-to-bottom sequence of links along which one or more predicate-predicate collapses are possible. Given that there are twice as many collapse routes in the new tree, the question arises as to whether the same systematic collapse patterns will occur in both trees. With the increase in possible routes it is possible that some collapses will be more haphazard and will violate the beads-on-a-string model. In short, the new tree provides a stronger test of the generality of the collapse patterns.

The third difference is that the pattern of some categories developing out of others is also tested more extensively with the new tree. Some of the evidence for this pattern was seen in cases where predicates moved down from a superordinate node in an asymmetrical manner. For example, when a child's tree represented a collapse between physical objects and events, the event predicates were only dimly understood, while the physical object predicates were clearly understood. Since the new tree provides many more cases in which both subordinate branches have predicates, there are more cases to examine for asymmetrical differentiation.

And fourth, the suggestion that terms denote their appropriate categories before unique predicates are correctly applied to those categories is tested more extensively by the new tree. Five out of six sets of terms now have unique predicates, whereas only two out of seven had unique predicates earlier. This increased number of unique predicates allows many more opportunities to test the hypothesis that terms denote categories before predicates.

In sum, the tree used in the second grade-school study was chosen because its general configurational properties were ideal for more extensive testing of all of the phenomena discovered in the first study. Attempts were also made to pick nodes that capture distinctions which might be related to other work in semantic and conceptual development.

Although in most respects the procedure was the same as that in the first study, certain changes and elaborations were made. The most important procedural change involved an expanded sequence of probe questions. This change sometimes resulted in as many as four sessions with a child before all predicates and terms could be tested. Sessions were conducted on successive schooldays if possible. Whenever practical, all probe questions conformed to a flow chart (Fig. 23).

This flow chart is best understood by means of concrete examples. The following interchanges represent two different paths taken through the flow chart for a five-year-old and a seven-year-old in response to questions about "The fight is skinny":

Five-year-old

E[xperimenter].   The fight is skinny.
C[hild].   That's O.K.
E.   How could a fight be skinny?
C.   Mm, not sure.
E.   Well, how could you tell if a fight was skinny?
C.   Oh, if the boys were skinny.
E.   Is it the boys that are skinny, or the fight, or both?
C.   Both.

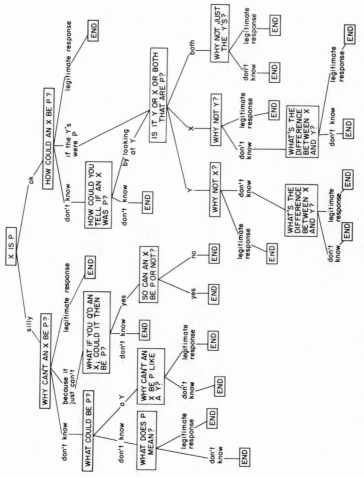

Figure 23. *Flow chart showing probe question procedure*

  E. Why not just the boys, or just the fight?
  C. Because they're both skinny. It's the same thing.

Seven-year-old
  E. The fight is skinny.
  C. That's silly.
  E. Why can't a fight be skinny?
  C. Because it just can't. That's impossible.
  E. What if you didn't feed a fight, could it then be skinny?
  C. No, fights just happen. You can feed people, but you can't even touch a fight.

Other routes through this chart that would follow from the same predicate-term pair are easy to imagine. The phrase "legitimate reply" refers to those cases where the child gave a reply that directly answered the question. The answer did not necessarily have to be the correct adult response but had simply to be unambiguous and to the point. For example, in the above two interchanges there are two legitimate responses, only one of which is the correct adult one. Thus, the five-year-old's last reply—("Because they're both skinny. It's the same thing")—was legitimate even though most adults do not feel that fights and people are the same thing. In the case of the seven-year-old, the legitimate response corresponded to a typical adult response.

In principle, every predicate-term combination should have been pursued to an end point in the chart. In practice, however, this was not always possible. Some children simply refused to continue with a given term or repeatedly went off on tangents. Occasionally children would spontaneously say something so interesting that the experimenter pursued it as a target of opportunity even if it departed from the tree. Even though such deviations from a standard question format are virtually inevitable with young children, most questioning sequences were in accordance with the flow chart.

The terminal end nodes do not necessarily mean that all questioning ceased for that topic. In fact, any end resulting from a "don't know" meant that the experimenter had to repeat the procedure with a new term or predicate.

It might seem that such an extensive probe questioning procedure would bias the children's answers. This effect is unlikely, since the usual effect of the extended probe questions was to ensure that the children's true intuitions and not response biases or other artifacts were being tapped. Nevertheless, the replies could have been biased, and if such an effect were to occur, the bias would most likely have made the children's responses more adult-like. Given the fact on the chart that children differ from adults only in that they judge certain anomalous sentences to be sensible and not vice versa, it is clear that probe questions about nonadult intuitions (the right half of the chart) were generally more exhaustive than those about adult-like intuitions (the left half of the chart). Thus, if there were any biasing effect of the questions, it would be to make children's trees more adult-like. Consequently, any developmental phenomena uncovered would be all the more convincing. In sum, the probe questions yield a conservative estimate of developmental patterns, and consequently any patterns that are found can be accepted with confidence.

There was a second, less important change in procedure. Instead of using half the terms with half the children and the other half with the remainder, the experimenter used the upper member of the term pairs in the new tree but was free to use a lower member if the child seemed more familiar with that term. This was done to maximize the chance that the child would be familiar with one of the two terms.

Finally, all children's responses were recorded and transcribed, generating six pages of coded transcripts for each child; probe questions and certain frequent phrases were abbreviated to reduce the number of transcript pages. Two investigators then independently constructed trees from the transcripts, referring back to the original recordings whenever necessary. Tree construction involved using a standard scoring procedure to interpret answers to probe questions as either "silly," "don't know," or "O.K." responses and then constructing trees according to the standard algorithm. Both scorers went through all transcripts at least two times to check their initial judgments. Spot-check reliabilities between the two scorers ranged between 94 and 100 percent agreement on responses. Virtually all disagreements were easily resolved through discussion, when it usually became readily apparent that one of the two scorers had misunderstood the response.

Sixteen children each in grades kindergarten, two, and four and ten sixth-graders participated in the study. Most children were from the white middle or upper classes. All children were from elementary schools in the Ithaca, New York area. Children whose first language was not English were permitted to participate in the study unless their abilities in English were so tentative as to create questions concerning their comprehension of probe questions. Using these criteria, two of the four children for whom English was a second language were dropped from the study.

The M Constraint

Trees were generated for all fifty-eight children (Figs. A57–A114 in Appendix C). As was the case in the first grade-school study, violations of the M constraint were extremely rare. There were only seven cases of trees with M-constraint violations, those of three kindergartners, one second-grader, two fourth-graders, and one sixth-grader. Since one of these trees (Fig. A99) contained two violations, there were eight M-constraint violations in all out of at least 100,000 possible occasions. The number of resolved ambiguities was twelve.

Because of the extensive probe questions, it is possible to take a closer look at the violations than was done in the first study. In particular, the question arises whether these violations actually represent a different semantic and conceptual structure or whether they are caused by other factors such as memory factors. The answers to the probes suggest the latter in that many M-constraint violations appear to be associated with children who are in a state of transition from one tree to a more developed one, and who occasionally forget what the new distinctions in the more mature tree are. The effect is that some of their intuitions are derived from the old knowledge structure and others from the new one, with the consequence that the intuitions themselves often result in M violations.

Support for the claim that most M violations are created by children who are in transition from one tree to another is evident in the type of answers given to probe questions. For example, one kindergartner (Fig. A72) made the following comments about "love" being "skinny":

E. Love is skinny.
C. Naah.
E. Why can't love be skinny?
C. Because love is fat, 100 percent fat.
E. One hundred percent fat?
C. Yeah.
E. How can love be fat?
C. Love is fat because—because fat is bigger and longer than skinny. Takes a longer time to hate the person than it is love—much, much longer.
E. How about love is tall?
C. Naah.

E.   Why can't love be tall?
C.   Love can't be tall. It can be wide but not tall.
E.   How could it be wide?
C.   If it was 100 yards long, that's how long it takes long to
     be. It can be long but not tall.

The same child made the following comments about a
"fight" being "skinny":

E.   The fight is skinny.
C.   No. The fight is long would be better.
E.   Why not skinny?
C.   No, fights can't be skinny—that's for sure.
E.   Why not?
C.   If there was no fight, it wouldn't be skinny at all. If there
     was a fight, it would be fat.
E.   How could a fight be fat?
C.   It would be fat if there was only one fat area to fight in,
     bunched up like a hamburger.
E.   Is it the fight or the area or both that are fat?
C.   Both.
E.   Why not just the area?
C.   'Cause if the area is fat, so is the fight.

These two interchanges suggest that this child is undergoing
a transition from a set of beliefs in which "fight" and "love"
denote physical objects to a system where they denote events.
The child shows a revealing confusion of the spatial and temporal aspects of "long," a phenomenon that is reminiscent of
Clark's (1973) theory about how temporal concepts develop
out of spatial ones.

The same transitional difficulty appears to be present in
most of the other trees that violate the M constraint. One
fourth-grader seemed to be confused about whether both
"love" and "idea" denoted events or abstract objects (Fig. A99).
The following experimenter-child interchange illustrates the
confusion:

E.   Love took a long time.
C.   That can make sense.
E.   How?
C.   For you to fall in love takes a long time.
E.   Is it the falling in love or love or both that take a long
     time?

C. Both.
E. Why not just the falling in love?
C. I don't know.
E. Love is near the school.
C. No, that's not sensible.
E. Why can't it be near a school?
C. It's a thing, but you can't see it. I can't explain it.
E. Could you trap it in a room?
C. No, it's not even like air. It's just a feeling inside you or
    something.
E. The idea took a long time.
C. Yes, that's O.K.
E. How could an idea take a long time?
C. Some inventors to come up with a good idea took a long
    time.
E. What took a long time, the coming up with it or the idea?
C. The idea.
E. Why not the coming up with it?
C. I don't know—maybe that too.
E. The idea is near the school.
C. Not really O.K.
E. Why not?
C. You can read near the school.
E. Yes, but why can't an idea be near a school.
C. You can think of it near the school, but the idea can't
    be near the school.
E. Why not?
C. Don't know how to explain it. It just doesn't fit in—its
    silly.

This child, actually appears to contradict himself in some of
the interchanges. Thus "idea" itself takes a long time, not just
the thinking of it, and yet just the thinking of it and not the
idea itself can be near the school.

This confused, often contradictory pattern of responses was
common to the M-constraint violators. Three violators in the
fourth and sixth grades (Figs. A99, A102, A107) appeared to
confuse abstract objects with events, while the other four violators in the second grade and kindergarten (Figs. A66, A69,
A72, A85) appeared to confuse physical objects with events.
These age-related differences in the apparent causes of the M-
constraint violations fit well the general developmental
progression suggested by the trees as a whole. That is, children

first learn to distinguish events from physical objects and only later abstract objects from events.

Several questions remain for future investigations. First, how common are M-constraint violations in any child's developmental history? Are they a regular indication of transition, seen only rarely in studies of this type because the transition is so rapid; or are they rare even for transitions? Second, how firmly entrenched are the M-constraint violations? Several of these children appeared to make outright contradictions. If confronted with their contradictions, would they stick to them or would they quickly agree that one intuition was wrong? A few children in this study were confronted with their contradictions after the session was complete, and in general they seemed to dismiss the contradiction by changing one of their answers. But these observations can only be anecdotal at this point. Further study is needed to determine the significance of M-constraint violations in the development of a given child's knowledge.

Four Representative Cases

One tree representing an immature five-year-old's intuitions was the simplest of all those generated, with only two categories of terms being distinguished: those that denote living things and those that denote everything else (Fig. 24; cf. Figs. A58, A59, A60, A61, A66). This child did not understand "about an x" or "true/false." She made the fairly common error of assuming that "about an x" meant "similar to an x" and ac-

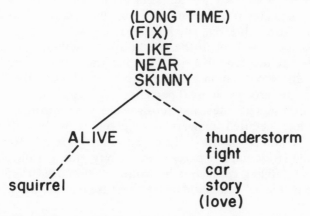

Figure 24. *Tree representing a five-year-old's intuitions*

cordingly answered that a thunderstorm could not be about a princess because "It isn't like a princess; it doesn't have a princess-like hat." Other answers appeared to be virtually random associations between the princess (or frog) and the term in question and did not even show consistent use of the notion "is similar to." The predicate "true" was taken to mean "real," but again not reliably.

The predicate "was x's fault" was also not understood. Answers showed little or no relation to the probes or were "don't knows." Thus, "The thunderstorm was x's fault" was judged "O.K." because "she told him something funny."

The predicate "fix" was at least partially understood with legitimate replies for stories, "You'd fix the pages," and cars, "You fix a car by taking it to a gas station and giving it to a car fixer." A squirrel could be fixed too. How? "With tools." What tools? "Screwdrivers." How would you use them on a squirrel? "Slowly." Moreover, the child stated that one fixed a squirrel just like a broken toy. "Fix" is in parentheses because the child also gave many "don't know" answers and irrelevant responses.

Both event predicates appeared to be systematically misunderstood so that they applied to all terms. For "took a long time" there appeared to be a triple ambiguity such that x could take a long time if x lasted a long time, x could take a long time if it took x a long time to do something, or x could take a long time if it took a long time to do something with x. Probe questions that pursued these answers, such as "Is it the car or the driving of the car that takes a long time, or both?" were usually met with "don't know" answers. This pattern of applying event predicates to all terms, but with uncertainty, was fairly common to all children, and it is debatable whether these predicates should be kept in the tree at all. Nonetheless, they are usually included in the trees to give the most information about children's responses. They are omitted when the "don't knows" are greater than 50 percent.

All other predicates and terms were very familiar to the child, and detailed answers were given to probes. Thus, a "story" could be "skinny" if the pages were skinny. Moreover, both the story and the pages were skinny, not just one or the other. A "fight" could not be "skinny" because "there's no people inside it," but could be fat "because it could fit two people in it."

In sum, it appears that this child could only distinguish living things from all other things. Moreover, the answers suggest that all other things were seen as physical objects that could be skinny or fat. The child appeared to have a clear idea of the difference between living things and other physical objects, as shown by comments that a car could not be alive since "it has a motor instead of blood," and love could not be alive "cause it has no stomach." The child may have had some vague preliminary understanding of events, but not enough to know either that event predicates could not apply to all things or, more important, that event terms could not denote things with physical dimensions.

Another tree represents the intuitions of a more advanced kindergartner (Fig. 25, A58). Trees of this sort were quite common among the kindergartners (Figs. A59, A66, A100). Two trees were virtually identical except that some different predicates and terms were used, which provides support for the argument that these trees represent more than a purely linguistic phenomenon (Figs. A60, A61).

For the more advanced kindergartner represented, "fix" was applied only to "car." The child was very clear on this point and answered questions about "fix" with conviction and good detail. In other children of the same age "fix" might also apply to "story" where "story" was taken to denote the book or the pages of the book.

In other respects this advanced child and many other kindergartners were like the immature child. "Is about x" and "true/false" were not understood, and the child showed considerable uncertainty with "was x's fault" and "long time." In addition, this particular child gave such a large number of "don't know" answers to questions about "love" that "love" is

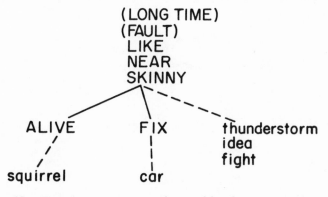

Figure 25. *Tree representing an advanced kindergartner's intuitions*

not shown in the tree. The most important common pattern is that again all terms could sensibly take physical object predicates. "Ideas" could be heavy or light and "fights" could be fat.

These patterns of acceptable predicate-term combinations strongly suggest a tripartite division of ontological categories into living things, functional artifacts, and other physical objects. The presence of the predicates "skinny/fat" and "tall/short" at the top of these trees argues for all objects being seen as physical. Children at this stage were also convinced that not all nonliving physical objects were fixable. Thus a thunderstorm could not be fixed "cause there's no metal in it."

Finally, some children at this age, as well as older children, used "fix" ambiguously. Not only could one fix a car, one could also fix love "by getting two people together again." But when asked if fixing love was the same as fixing a car, most children emphatically stated that it was a very different kind of fixing because, as one second-grader put it, "you use a screwdriver for a car, but *not* for love! That would be silly."

Another tree representing the intuitions of a second-grader showed a pattern quite common to children of this older age group (Fig. 26, A77). In general, the second-graders as a group were the most interesting, for the trees seemed to undergo the greatest degree of change during this period. Many second-graders demonstrated for the first time an awareness of non-physical categories.

The second-grader represented was quite certain of most of her judgments and rarely hesitated in her responses. The predicate "skinny" could be applied only to terms that denoted physical objects for adults ("squirrels" and "cars"), and the event predicates could be sensibly applied to both terms that denoted events and terms that denoted abstract objects, but

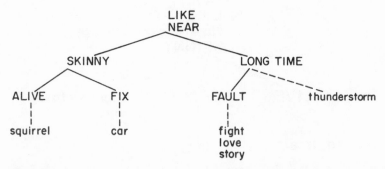

Figure 26.   *Tree representing a second-grader's intuitions*

not to terms that denoted physical objects. A "story" could take a "long time" "if it was a long story," but "the car took a long time" "doesn't make much sense . . . could make sense . . . in a way if . . . somebody could be driving it and have trouble starting it . . . not just the car." When asked if a car could be an hour long, the child responded, "Silly, hours doesn't measure a car." Similarly, a "squirrel" could not be an hour long because "you can't measure it by that."

This child's answers strongly suggested that abstract objects such as stories and love were seen as events and not as other types of nonphysical things. This can be seen not only in the application of event predicates to "love" and "story" but also in certain spontaneous answers to questions about physical-object predicates being combined with these terms. For example, when asked if "love" could be "skinny," this child emphatically said, "No; love is a thing that two people do together." Similar answers suggesting a conception of love as an event were given to questions about the predicates "fix" and "alive." Analogous responses were given to questions about stories suggesting a conception of the story as an event in which the story is communicated.

Finally, this child, as well as several others in this age group, would apply "was x's fault" or "was on purpose" only to the terms "love," "fight," and "story" and not to "thunderstorms," "squirrels," or "cars." A squirrel could not be on purpose "because things on purpose have to be things you do." Or an event such as a thunderstorm could not be on purpose since "people don't know when a thunderstorm comes." These answers indicate an awareness of the distinction between intentional and naturally occurring events where certain abstract objects are conceived of as intentional events.

This child represented a common pattern among second-graders, a major division into the three ontological categories of living things (perhaps actually animals), functional artifacts, and events. Events were further divided into intentional and naturally occurring events. Abstract objects were generally conceived of as intentional events, a pattern that was also quite common among second-graders; in fact there were nine second-graders who appeared to treat abstract objects as intentional events. A few second-graders treated thunderstorms as intentional events but did seem to understand the concept. They posited intentional causes of thunderstorms such as God or "somebody who knows magic."

One unusual case of making an abstract object an intentional event occurred with a second-grader (Fig. A82). This child would use "about *x*" only with "idea" and at the same time still thought an idea to be a type of intentional event. When asked if a squirrel could be about a princess, the child responded that it was silly since "stories are sometimes about princesses and plays are about princesses, but not squirrels." Why not? "Because squirrels can't be about a princess unless you dump a lot of squirrels on top of her, and that's different!" This child spontaneously mentioned two other types of propositional information that "about *x*" could apply to even though she had not yet been asked about ideas and was never asked about stories or plays.

Despite this apparent understanding of "about," this child nevertheless seemed to think of ideas as special kinds of events that embodied information. Thus she said, "If an idea was a special kind of idea, then it might take a long time to make up." When asked if it was the idea or the making up that took a long time, the child replied that it was both; but she could only reply when asked, "Why isn't it just the making up?" with "Because it just isn't."

A large number of second-graders had a great deal of difficulty with "about *x*" and "true/false," and high incidences of "don't knows" often forced exclusion of these predicates from their trees. The unusual child described may have been in a more advanced stage where she was just about to make the transition to conceiving of ideas as abstract objects. Other second-graders also appeared to have a beginning understanding of what sorts of things "about *x*" could be applied to. Thus one child (Fig. A84) stated that a thunderstorm could not be about a frog because "it's not like a story . . . 'cause it's not about anything . . . you can't read a thunderstorm."

One final individual tree representing the intuitions of a fourth-grader again was quite typical for children in this age group (Figs. 27, A105). This child appeared to have a clearer notion of the predicate "is about *x*," as he would combine it only with the term "story" and indicated through his answers that other things could not be "about *x*" because they were not story-like things ("Love can't be about a princess, love isn't a story").

This child differed from adults in only one respect: the term "love" is spanned by "was an hour long," "was Johnny's fault," and "near the school." None of these predicates span "love" for most adults. This pattern of intuitions, as well as the answers to probe questions, suggest that the child felt that love denoted

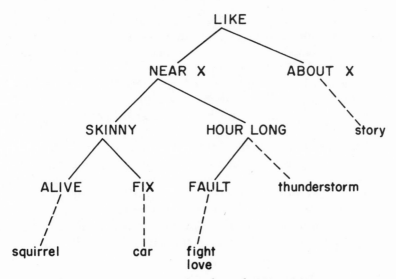

Figure 27.   *Tree representing a fourth-grader's intuitions*

an intentional event. Thus love could be on purpose if "somebody wanted love so bad they started it." Started what? "Love." When asked if love would take a long time, this child said that it could because it could take a long time for two people to love each other. This predicate was not seen as inappropriate for love. Perhaps the most dramatic evidence for fourth-graders still conceiving of love as an event comes from another fourth-grader who, when asked if love could take a long time, stated, "Naw, it's just an action. It couldn't take years and years" (Fig. A94). This child did think it could take a shorter amount of time.

It was quite common for fourth-graders to treat love as an event; seven out of sixteen did so, some making it an intentional event, others making it a natural event by arguing that people have no control over it and that "it just happens." This development frequently appears to be the last one before a fully mature tree emerges. More advanced fourth-graders generally moved "love" up in the tree so that it was spanned only by "like." Thus, most of the sixth-graders had adult trees.

Developmental Patterns Reconsidered

One of the purposes of this follow-up study was to test in a more stringent manner the validity of the tentative developmental patterns suggested by the first grade-school study. The results provide strong support for all those phenomena.

With respect to increased differentiation, the increases with age in the mean number of term categories were similar to those found in the first study. The means were 3.4 for the kindergartners, 4.3 for the second-graders, 5.2 for the fourth-graders, and 5.5 for the sixth-graders. These age increases were significant as a group (analysis of variance, $p < .01$) and individually, except for the fourth- to sixth-graders change (Scheffé test, $p < .05$).

As in the case of the first study, the immature trees were collapsed in a systematic manner. Thus, there was only one case where a predicate moved down the tree to form a collapse (Fig. A63). The child apparently had a different meaning for "skinny," such that it could be applied only to animals.

Inverse dominance relations were even rarer than in the first study. There were no such inversions in either kindergarten or

Inverse Domination

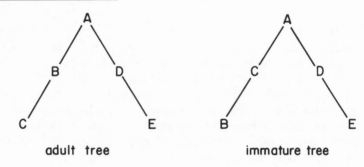

Lateral Movement

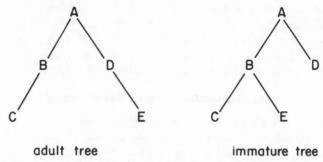

Figure 28. *Trees showing inverse dominance and lateral movement*

second-grade subjects, and only three in the fourth- and sixth-graders. Given that there were more than one thousand possible inverse dominance relations, such a small incidence is negligible. This does not mean, however, that all kindergarten and second-grade trees strictly followed the beads-on-a-string model. There were a few immature trees in which a predicate on a different branch was moved over laterally. Inverse dominance differs from this type of violation (Fig. 28).

There were nine instances of lateral movement: two, three, four, and zero instances in grades kindergarten, two, four, and six, respectively. Given the large number of possible lateral movements, or 1160, these instances are clearly minor deviations from a predominant pattern.

In sum, the so-called "beads on a string" constraint on tree development appears to be a strong restriction which the vast majority of immature trees honors.

At the ontological level this pattern can now be more confidently interpreted as evidence for increasing awareness of more and more ontological categories. Experimenter-child interchanges of the type described lend support to the claim that what develops is not only an awareness of the meanings of certain lexical items but also an awareness of deeper conceptual distinctions.

With regard to the pattern of ordered and asymmetric differentiation the percentages of children whose intuitions re-

Table 12 *Collapses of adjacent predicates in second grade-school study*

	Grade			
Collapse	K	2	4	6
LIKE/NEAR	93%	93%	44%	10%
NEAR/SKINNY	37%	13%	0%	0%
SKINNY/ALIVE	6%	0%	0%	0%
SKINNY/FIX	6%	0%	0%	0%
NEAR/AN HOUR LONG[a]	83%	44%	6%	10%
	$n = 12$			
AN HOUR LONG/FAULT[a]	80%	9%	0%	0%
	$n = 5$			
LIKE/ABOUT X[a]	0%	0%	0%	0%
	$n = 0$			

a. Several younger children were unfamiliar with one or both of the predicates in these pairs.

sulted in a particular collapse decreased at each age, if all possible adjacent predicate-predicate collapses are considered (Table 12). There is some difficulty in interpreting the unfamiliar predicate pairs, as not all children knew enough about the relevant predicates or terms to have them in their trees. For this reason those percentages, especially for "one hour long" versus "fault" and "like" versus "about x," should be interpreted with caution. There nonetheless appears to be good evidence for an ordered differentiation of predicates.

The order appeared roughly as follows:

1. skinny/alive
2. skinny/fix
3. near/skinny
4. near/an hour long
5. like/near

Pairs containing "fault" and "about x" are omitted from this ordering because there were so many "don't know" answers about these predicates in the younger children. This ordering suggests a corresponding ordering of ontological categories as follows:

Ontological distinction	Corresponding predicate pair
1. living things/other physical objects	skinny/alive
2. functional artifacts/other physical objects	skinny/fix
3. events/physical objects	near/skinny, near an hour long
4. events/abstract objects	like/near

Answers by the children suggested that the distinction between natural and intentional events was probably attained at a point shortly after the "events" versus "physical objects" distinction. Thus in more than 90 percent of those cases where "long time" or "an hour long" isolated terms denoting events, "was x's fault" or "on purpose" also made the distinction between intentional and natural events. Moreover, "was x's fault" and "was on purpose" virtually never marked this latter distinction before "long time" and "an hour long" marked the more general distinction between events and physical objects.

The collapses also give some indication of the asymmetry of predicate differentiation. For example, "near x" versus "skinny" became differentiated before "near" versus "an hour long." This suggests that the child knew first that there were physical objects and something else, but only later that the something else was events. Therefore, as in the case of the first grade-school study, asymmetrical differentiation can be interpreted as a sign that categories differentiate out of other prior ones and not out of syncretic wholes.

The data as a whole suggest the following sequence of categories developing "out of" others:

1. physical objects
2. living objects out of nonliving physical objects
3. functional artifacts out of other nonliving physical objects
4. events out of physical objects
5. intentional events out of natural events
6. abstract objects out of events

The four sample trees of grade-school children illustrate how answers to probe questions strongly suggest a sequence of this type. Some parts of the sequence are more speculative than others, however. For example, it is not clear whether intentional events arise out of natural events or whether both types of events are discerned as soon as events in general are understood. If the latter alternative were true, then the prior general concept "event" would probably be syncretic in nature.

There was also support for the pattern of terms denoting categories before predicates. A term or set of terms would frequently represent a separate node and yet not have a unique predicate. Thus, for example, event terms frequently denoted a separate category while the predicate "an hour long" was still at a higher node. Similarly "story" and "idea" were frequently set aside as separate categories before the predicate "about x" uniquely spanned them.

In sum, the results of the second elementary school study provide strong support for all of the patterns suggested by the first grade-school study. In addition, there is tentative evidence for two new patterns, lateral shifts in terms and transitional states.

Because the tree used in the follow-up study had more lateral branches and less top-down embeddings, it was possible to see more clearly a pattern only hinted at by the first study. Terms in immature trees would sometimes be displaced laterally so as to be dominated by predicates on entirely different branches. This pattern is closely related to the proposed underlying phenomena of categories developing out of others. Thus, abstract object terms frequently were shifted laterally into positions dominated by event predicates. For example, "love" and "fear" were frequently spanned by the predicate for intentional events. Similarly, terms for events sometimes shifted laterally so that they were dominated by physical-object predicates. Occasionally a shift would occur where not only a term but also its unique predicate would be moved. Thus, in two cases, "about x" moved with "story," so as to be dominated by event predicates. This pattern is simply a different way of viewing what seems to be the underlying developmental phenomenon, that new ontological categories develop out of old ones.

The extensive probe questioning also revealed cases where children appeared to be halfway between two tree structures. These transitional states were marked by high degrees of uncertainty in responses and by M structures. Future study is needed to understand better how changes in knowledge are responsible for tree differentiation.

The Preschool Study

The evidence for the generality of developmental patterns and for the underlying ontological development leads to the question of earlier origins. It has been shown that kindergartners honor the M constraint and that their trees are already somewhat differentiated. Do younger children also honor the M constraint? Do they even have intuitions that enable one to generate trees? A study with preschoolers was conducted to answer these questions.

Preschoolers are not especially amenable to prolonged interview sessions. For this reason a more informal study was conducted. A research associate became involved in a local nursery school for several weeks prior to the study. She helped out with the various chores and was soon accepted by the children as just another adult caretaker. While parents and preschool staff were informed of the study, the children themselves were not even aware that they were in a study. The research associate collected data by casually taking a child aside and asking questions for a few moments. Children might be seen more than ten times over several days before a complete set of intuitions was obtained.

An abbreviated tree structure was used with the younger

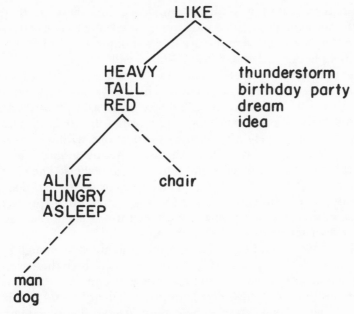

Figure 29. *Predicability tree used in preschool study*

children in order to increase the chance of obtaining a complete set of intuitions (Fig. 29). The tree was based on only three categories: animals, other physical objects, and nonphysical objects.

As in the elementary-school studies, children were asked if certain predicate pairs sounded silly. In many cases it seemed more effective to ask questions in the form of, "Could a *t* be *P*?" so this variation was frequently used. Predicates and their opposites were used to check on plausibility versus possibility. Probe question sequences roughly followed the elementary-school flow chart (Fig. 23), although the preschool sequences were usually considerably less extensive. Tests for ambiguity were not explicitly made, although sometimes an ambiguity became apparent during questioning. It was rarely possible to collect a complete set of justified judgments about all predicate-term pairs; nevertheless, enough judgments were normally collected to enable the construction of trees.

Nine subjects participated, ranging in age from 3 years 2 months to 4 years 9 months. The mean age was 4 years 1 month. The majority of subjects came from families in which both parents worked.

With six of the nine preschoolers it was possible to construct a tree representation. With the remaining three children, there were not enough justified judgments to be able to construct a tree. The six trees were remarkably similar to each other, five of them being variants of one tree (Fig. 30).

These five trees were variants in that not all predicates and terms were used with each child. Thus, for a particular child "dog" might be dominated by "hungry" and "asleep" while the terms "alive" and "man" were not tested. In all five cases, however, there were two term categories: one with a term or terms denoting animals, the other with terms denoting both nonliving physical objects and nonphysical objects. The sixth tree contained three categories represented by the terms "dog," "chair," and "thunderstorm." "Birthday party" also appeared to be at the same location as "thunderstorm," but in this case the responses were somewhat sparse.

The three remaining children simply did not give enough responses to be able to construct full trees. In all three there were some indications of a distinction between terms denoting animals and other things. For example, a "chair" could not be hungry but a "dog" could. The usual cause for incomplete answers was a failure on the child's part to answer probe questions. In other cases children simply refused to continue the session after a very short period of time.

If all nine sets of responses are analyzed for evidence of intersecting sets of terms, no such evidence is found. This is strong support for the view that these children honored the M con-

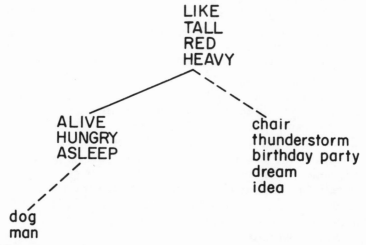

Figure 30. *Tree representing intuitions in preschool study*

straint. Of course, with only three nodes, the ratio of potential structures that violate the M constraint to those that do not is considerably smaller than for trees with seven nodes. Nevertheless, the probability of obtaining, by chance, only arrays that honor the M constraint is still extremely small ($p < .001$). Further support for the claim that these children honored the M constraint comes from the fact that on several occasions two or even three predicates were used at the same node ("alive," "hungry," "asleep"). Such multiple cases of predicates and terms at one node clearly increase the probability of an M-constraint violation occurring by chance.

Beyond providing further support for the M constraint, the cases of multiple predicates or terms also provide evidence for a strong underlying conceptual influence on the child's understanding of term meanings. It was almost always the case that if one predicate failed to mark an adult distinction, other predicates at the same node in the adult tree would also fail to mark the distinction. Thus, if a "thunderstorm" was tall, it was also "heavy" and "red." If the trees were collapsed simply because the child had assigned the wrong meaning to one particular predicate, then one would not expect the other predicates to exhibit the same mistake. Similarly, using the same example, it was extremely unlikely that the collapse was merely a consequence of misunderstanding the meaning of the word "thunderstorm" since the terms "birthday party" and "dream" were also systematically misunderstood in the same way; that is, they all took physical object predicates.

This last point reinforces the notion that the collapsed predicate-term trees represent corresponding collapses in ontological knowledge. Thus, for five of the six children for whom trees were constructed, all things appeared to be categorized as physical objects of two kinds: living and nonliving. However, although these children classified all things as physical objects, they did not all necessarily make an abstract object the same type of physical object. In fact, there was enormous variation among the children in how they made abstract objects physical, a point that is of importance.

The following two interchanges illustrate very different ways of making dreams physical objects. The first child was 4 years 2 months:

E. Can dreams be tall?
C. Yeah.
E. How tall?

C. Big, Big, big [spreads arms].
E. Where are dreams?
C. In your bedroom.
E. In the daytime?
C. No, they're outside.
E. Could you see a dream?
C. Yeah.
E. How?
C. They're red.
E. What are they like?
C. They're made out of rock.
E. Could they be heavy?
C. Yeah, and they can't break either.
E. What do they look like?
C. They look like rocks. Like they're asleep on the grass. And the kids go outside and they see the dream things asleep.
E. Are dreams alive then?
C. No, they're not dead either. They just got grass on them.

This was the only case in which "asleep" and "alive" did not share the same node. The second child was 4 years 5 months:

E. Can dreams be tall?
C. Yes, tall.
E. How can they be tall?
C. This tall [stretches hands up].
E. What are they like?
C. They're like clouds with pictures too.
E. Are they just like clouds?
C. Yes.
E. Where do dreams go during the day?
C. They turn white and go up in the sky.

Clearly the only constraint is that dreams be physical objects, while within that constraint all sorts of objects are likely candidates.

In sum, the preschool study provides evidence, first, that the children do seem to honor the M constraint. Second, they appear, at least implicitly, to have knowledge that results in a distinction between implausible and nonsensical concepts. Third, they distinguish animals from other things. Finally, the patterns of collapses of multiple predicates and terms at the same node suggest a lack of both linguistic knowledge and ontological knowledge.

A Study in a Different Language

In an attempt to test further the generality of the developmental findings, a study was conducted with Spanish-speaking children in Puerto Rico. While Spanish is more closely related to English than are many other languages, there are nevertheless some differences between the two languages that provide a stronger test of the theory than if it were tested solely in English. For example, Spanish has more variable relations in predicate-term order, and different syntactic means are sometimes used to express the same concepts in the two languages. This type of variability reduces the likelihood that inferred developmental changes in conceptual knowledge reflect only changes in syntactic competence. The Spanish study is thus a small step in the direction of testing the universal properties of ontological knowledge and its development.

There are also moderate cultural differences between the Puerto Rican children and the English-speaking children tested earlier. One difference of possible relevance is that the Puerto Rican children tended to come from deeply religious families in a semirural region of Puerto Rico and that many of these families held superstitious beliefs different from those held by Americans. Such differences might result in different conceptions of the world and hence different ontological structures.

An adult Spanish tree was used as a source of stimulus sentences (Fig. 31). This tree is in the rural Puerto Rican dialect and consequently differs somewhat from European Spanish. The tree was constructed by a Spanish-English bilingual who had grown up in Puerto Rico. An English tree was used as a model (Fig. 32) but substitution of different predicates and terms was allowed if the substituted term or predicate seemed more natural in Puerto Rican. An additional constraint was that all predicates and terms should be understandable to young Puerto Rican children.

After the Puerto Rican tree was constructed, several other native Puerto Ricans were consulted to see if they agreed on the terms and predicates and also if they agreed on sensibleness judgments. Some changes were made when it was found that a given term or predicate was ambiguous. Finally, the method of back-translation was used whereby another bilingual translated the Puerto Rican tree back into English to see if indeed the two trees were comparable. The back-translation was suc-

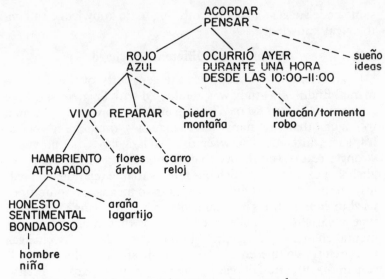

Figure 31. *Spanish tree used in Puerto Rican study*

cessful in generating a tree that had the same predicates and terms as the English tree drawn up by the first translator.

The procedure was essentially the same as that used in the second grade-school study. The investigator used a similar probe-questioning technique (Fig. 23).

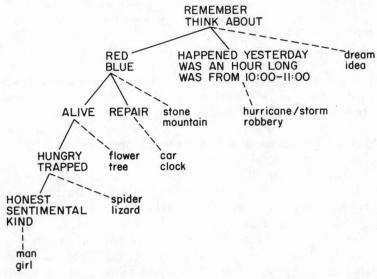

Figure 32. *English translation of tree used in Puerto Rican study*

All subjects were native Spanish-speaking children who knew little or no English. They all lived in south-central Puerto Rico near the city of Ponce. Fifteen children at each of three grades—kindergarten, first, and third—participated as subjects.

The trees for the children have all been translated into English for ease of interpretation (Figs. A115–A159 in Appendix C). In general the data were remarkably similar to those found in the two studies with English-speaking children.

Children at all ages honored the M constraint. Only two violations each were seen in the kindergartners, the first-graders, and the third-graders. Even in these cases there seemed to be possible ambiguities, such as "repair" meaning "heal" as well as "fix." Clearly, then, the M constraint holds in Puerto Rican children at all the ages studied.

With regard to the pattern of increased differentiation, there was a regular increase with age in the mean number of term categories per tree. Thus there were 3.9 categories for kindergartners, 4.1 categories for first-graders, and 5.2 categories for third-graders. These increases are quite similar to those found in the two studies with English-speaking elementary-school children.

As in the English language studies, immature trees were collapsed in a systematic manner. Predicates were rarely in inverse dominance relations, such as "alive" dominating "red." There were only two cases of a single inversion and one case of a double inversion among the kindergartners, one single inversion among the first-graders, and two single inversions among the third-graders. Lateral movements were also rare, with only two instances in the kindergartners and no instances in other grades.

The general pattern for predicates moving down the tree with development to span decreasing sets of terms was repeated in this study. There was, however, some exception to this general rule with the predicate "vivo" (alive) which was below its normal adult position in three kindergarten trees, nine first-grade trees, and five third-grade trees. In all these cases "vivo" spanned only animal terms and no longer spanned plant terms. There were no other instances of predicates being below their normal position in immature trees. While such instances were much rarer in English, amounting to one or two cases per study, they usually involved the predicate "alive."

It is not clear how important this difference is between the two languages. It may be an early indication that the pattern of predicates moving down with development is not as general as was first thought; or somewhat more likely it may be simply a consequence of "alive" being subtly ambiguous, with one meaning for both animals and plants and the other for just animals. Future work is needed to clarify this issue. If "alive" is ambiguous, it might explain why the first-graders actually made more "mistakes" than either the kindergartners or third-graders. The kindergartners may have two different meanings for "alive," one for animals and one for plants. In contrast, the first-graders may realize that there should be just one meaning and tend to adopt the meaning for animals; consequently they appear to make more mistakes than kindergartners. Only later, in the third-grade do children begin to use the more biological meaning of "alive" and correctly apply it to both plants and animals. Carey (forthcoming) has proposed a very similar account of how the meaning of "alive" is acquired.

With regard to the pattern of ordered and asymmetric differentiation, the percentages of children whose trees contained collapses between any two adjacent predicates (Table 13) decreased with increasing age. In some cases the percentages are unreliable, since only a small number of children were well enough acquainted with the two predicates so as to have them both included in their trees. That is, if a child gave a high incidence of "don't know" responses to probe questions about a

Table 13   Collapses of adjacent predicates in Puerto Rican study

	Grade		
Collapse	K	1	3
HUNGRY/HONEST	20%	16%	9%
	n = 5	n = 6	n = 11
HUNGRY/ALIVE	85%	43%	53%
	n = 13	n = 14	n = 15
ALIVE/REPAIR	0%	0%	0%
	n = 5	n = 9	n = 13
ALIVE/RED	0%	0%	0%
	n = 15	n = 15	n = 15
REPAIR/RED	20%	11%	8%
	n = 5	n = 9	n = 13
RED/REMEMBER	73%	27%	7%
	n = 15	n = 15	n = 15
HAPPENED YESTERDAY/REMEMBER	63%	55%	27%
	n = 8	n = 9	n = 11

Table 14 *Collapses of selected term pairs*[a]

	Grade		
Collapse[b]	K	1	3
LIZARD/GIRL	60%	67%	47%
GIRL/CAR	7%	7%	0%
LIZARD/TREE	33%	0%	13%
LIZARD/ROCK	13%	0%	0%
TREE/CAR	31%	21%	13%
CAR/ROCK	77%	43%	20%
TREE/ROCK	33%	62%	27%
ABSTRACT OBJECT TERM/EVENT TERM	58%	64%	47%
ABSTRACT OBJECT TERM/PHYSICAL OBJECT TERM	42%	47%	7%
EVENT TERM/PHYSICAL OBJECT TERM	33%	21%	13%

a. n's ranged from 13 to 15; most were 15.

b. For either the term shown or its alternate when used instead (e.g. "spider" instead of "lizard").

specific predicate, that predicate was not included in the tree. While this also occurred in the studies with English-speaking children, it was more frequent with the Puerto Rican children. This higher incidence is most likely a consequence of two related procedural factors: a less extensive piloting of vocabulary items and a lack of access to any published norms about vocabularies of young Puerto Rican children.

Because of this higher incidence of unfamiliarity with certain predicates, the predicate-predicate collapses, while helpful, are not sufficient to give a clear picture of the ordered differentiation of categories. For this reason, selected term-term collapses were also evaluated (Table 14). As in the English studies, children had much less difficulty with term meanings, so there were few cases of terms being omitted from the trees. Although similar term-term collapse tables were constructed for the English language studies and suggest the same order of differentiation as does the corresponding analysis of predicates, they have not been shown, since the predicate-predicate collapse data in those studies illustrate the orderings well and in addition offer a more parsimonious and revealing way of summarizing results.

From these two tables the following order of ontological categories may be inferred:

Ontological distinction	Corre-sponding predicate pair	Corresponding term pairs
1. living/nonliving	alive/red	lizard /rock girl / car
2. plants/animals	alive/hungry	lizard /tree girl /
3. events/physical objects	an hour long/ remember	hurricane /any physical robbery / object
4. functional arti-facts/other physical objects	repair/red	car/rock
5. plants/other physical objects	alive/red	tree/rock
6. abstract objects/ events or physical objects	—	dream /any event or idea / physical object
7. humans/other animals	honest/ hungry	lizard/girl

The relative order of some adjacent categories, such as 5 before 6, is almost arbitrary, especially since there are no data on children older than third grade. But ordering relations are more significant between nonadjacent categories, such as 3 before 5 or 5 before 7. This ordering is compatible with that found in the prior two studies. The main difference seems to be a later development in the Puerto Rican children of the distinction between functional artifacts and other physical objects. Why this should be the case is difficult to explain; it may be due to some subtle difference in the meaning of "repair" across the two languages.

Again the pattern of terms denoting categories before predicates emerged, characteristically with event and abstract-object terms being isolated in the tree while their unique predicates were still clustered at higher nodes common to other categories. This pattern is similar to that seen in the English elementary-school studies.

One interesting aspect of this pattern was that the younger children had difficulty with the event predicates and often said that they could be applied sensibly to all things. The same children were also generally less certain in their answers to probe questions about such material. The parallels between the two

languages are striking, in that in both cases children had difficulty with event predicates and tended to put them at the top
node in the tree. This was done even though the syntactic
forms of the event predicates and the lexical items varied between the two languages. These facts lend credence to the
claim, already supported by answers to probe questions, that
the children were not letting event predicates apply to all
terms simply because of some syntactically used ellipsis. Instead, the children's difficulty with the event predicates
seemed to be at a conceptual level.

The second elementary-school study led to the discovery of
lateral shifts and transitional states in tree development, and
some evidence of such phenomena can also be found in the
Puerto Rican study. However, because the model Spanish tree
did not have extensive left-to-right branching and since a detailed exposition of the probe questioning presents translation
problems, the relevant material is not presented here.

In sum, it is clear that the M constraint and the general developmental patterns hold for the Spanish-speaking children
who have been studied. The similarities between the data for
Spanish-speaking and English-speaking children were dramatic. Two differences that might appear to a larger extent in
other languages and cultures were a different ordering of category differentiation and a movement of some predicates up the
tree instead of down as development proceeds.

The three follow-up studies provide strong support for the
conclusions of the initial developmental study and answer
some of the questions raised by that study. The M constraint
appears to be an extremely strong principle that exerts its influence over trees at any stage of development, even in preschoolers. The general developmental patterns suggested by
the initial study appeared repeatedly in the two follow-up studies with elementary-school children. These patterns therefore
appear to be quite robust.

In addition to demonstrating the replicability of the previous
findings, the three additional studies made clearer the fact that
the trees represent more than mere linguistic phenomena. Use
of different syntactic formats and a different language had little
effect on the patterns of development. Similarly, neither general tree configurations nor particular nodes appeared to be responsible for either the M constraint or the patterns of development. Instead—and this notion was clearly bolstered by the
answers to the more extensive probe questions—the trees ap-

pear to represent growth of an underlying conceptual knowledge of ontological categories, a knowledge that is intricately
linked to language use via predicability but which seems to be
the original source of predicability phenomena.

As always, these new findings bring up new questions or
clarify older questions. Among the most difficult questions
that remain are: why do the M constraint and the specific developmental patterns exist, and what mechanisms enable a
child's knowledge to change in the manner described by the
trees? They require a good deal more empirical as well as theoretical inquiry.

8 | Other Developmental Research

F OUR STUDIES now point toward the same account of how ontological knowledge develops. There can be little doubt that they characterize a reliable and robust developmental phenomenon. These findings relate to other research on the development of cognition and language in a variety of ways. Not only are there few incompatibilities between this and prior research, but in some cases the theory of ontological knowledge may even help to explain previous findings by means of a broader and more coherent theoretical framework. The earlier relevant developmental work is concerned with anomaly, word meaning, Piagetian realisms, metaskills, causal thinking, animism, classification skills, and hierarchical knowledge.

Anomaly

Has it been shown in other studies that young children have intuitions about semantic anomaly? Do their intuitions differ from those of adults? If differences exist, are they of the same type as those found in the four developmental studies? Unfortunately developmental research on anomaly has not been sufficiently detailed to supply complete answers to all of these questions. Nonetheless, some comparisons are possible.

One study that specifically investigated the development of intuitions about selection restrictions was conducted by James and Miller (1973). They found that younger children, while sensitive to some selection restrictions, are not sensitive to others, a general result that is compatible with the four developmental studies. Their stimuli consisted exclusively of violations of human/nonhuman and animate/inanimate distinctions. In addition, some of their "anomalies," such as "the furry girl," would not be considered true category mistakes. For these reasons, it is not possible to make meaningful detailed comparisons between their results and those of the four developmental studies. James and Miller did, however, find different levels of performance for different syntactic forms. Adjective-noun anomalies, for example, are picked up less frequently by four-and-a-half year olds than are subject-predicate anomalies. This finding helps to emphasize the need for using a variety of syntactic forms in future studies.

In a similar vein, Howe and Hillman (1973) have investigated the development of the child's awareness of what they call "semantic restrictions." Their results are roughly comparable to those of James and Miller, namely that younger children, while sensitive to some anomalies, are not sensitive to others. Again there is insufficient detail to make precise comparisons between their results and those obtained in the four developmental studies.

A number of investigators have focused on the child's awareness of semantic anomaly as a metalinguistic skill. In general, these investigators ask whether the young child has an explicit awareness of semantic anomaly as opposed to other forms of linguistic irregularity. In the four developmental studies, children were never explicitly asked to make this distinction; rather it was inferred, by use of polar opposites, that children were judging anomaly and not falsehood. If, however, young children can make explicit judgments about anomaly, such a finding would provide additional support for the claim that they have an awareness of distinct ontological categories.

The evidence that children as young as three have such a metalinguistic skill is strong. Gleitman et al. (1974) observed that young children are able to distinguish anomaly from falsehood. Similarly, Devilliers and Devilliers (1972, 1974) report cases where young children are capable of making judgments of semantic anomaly. By contrast, these same children are often unable to make judgments of syntactic acceptability, which brings up the issue of whether intuitions are an accurate measure of underlying competence. In the case of syntax, as the Devilliers (1978) point out, correct intuitions about grammaticality lag far behind correct use of the same grammatical structures. Is it possible that the same lag is occurring between predicate-term usage and judgments of semantic anomaly? Perhaps children honor certain semantic restrictions in their productions at a considerably earlier age than that at which they can make correct judgments about them. If such a lag were to exist, then one might wonder whether intuitions about sense and nonsense were valid measures of underlying conceptual organization.

Such a possibility is unlikely. One reason has to do with the notion of accessibility. Gleitman and Gleitman (1978) argue that of all the metalinguistic intuitions, those about semantics are by far the most accessible and immediate. This high degree of accessibility means that as soon as children honor a semantic restriction in language use, they should be able to make judgments about violations of that restriction. Informal support for this claim comes from the fact that children who judge an anomaly to be appropriate almost invariably produce such anomalies in their speech. Witness some of the answers given to probe questions. This, of course, is in marked contrast to the lag between syntactically correct productions and judgments about correct syntax.

In fact, it is difficult to imagine how children could have an awareness of semantic restrictions and yet not think certain sentences to be anomalous. When children exhibit such a lag with syntax, the problem might be explained by saying that they look through the syntax and make judgments about the meaning; that is, they are unable to use the metalinguistic skill of stepping back and looking at syntax in itself. But it is difficult to imagine what children could "look at" that is beyond meaning. If children are able to comprehend a sentence, it would seem to be necessary that they look at its meaning. Thus, if children can understand certain predicate-term combinations, they should also be able to make judgments about their semantic sense.

Word Meaning

Recently, there have been a large number of studies on the growth of word meanings, most of which have focused on the growth of individual lexical items. Such research is of interest for two reasons. First, one can ask whether general developmental patterns in the acquisition of word meanings are related to the growth of predicability trees. Second, one can ask how studies and theories on the development of particular semantic domains, such as temporal terms, might be related to the development of certain ontological categories, such as events.

In the first case, one pattern frequently mentioned in the literature is that of overextension. Clark (1973) has proposed that the acquisition of many word meanings proceeds by a process of adding more and more semantic features to the definition of a word. Because young children have only part of the total adult complement of features, they apply the word to a wider range of objects; this practice is called overextension. Clark argues that, as development proceeds, the child adds more and more features and overextends less and less. As evidence for this proposal, she points to a variety of diary and observational studies containing examples of overextension.

Clark's theory has been criticized on the grounds that she overlooks underextension (Anglin, 1975, 1977). The argument is made that if one looks simply at production, the overextensions are often highly conspicuous because of their deviance from adult conventions, but underextensions would never be noted because the child simply remains silent. Anglin, using a variety of techniques, claims that children actually undergeneralize more than twice as much as they overgeneralize. In another example, Bloom (1973) observed that her own child used "car" to apply only to moving cars.

The issue of overextensions and underextensions relates to the four developmental studies in that they demonstrate overextensions of various predicates. For example, many children in the developmental studies extended "is sorry" to animals and occasionally even to plants. Even more important, the tree structure makes it possible to tell if underextensions occurred. Those would have been cases where a child moved a predicate down the tree below its adult node, which hardly ever occurred. Therefore, underextension is a rare phenomenon, at least for the predicates used in these studies. In theory one could argue that all the terms were being systematically underextended and that the predicates were being used appropriately, but such an argument is hardly plausible, besides being highly unparsimonious.

The terms in the four studies were rarely overextended. In most cases, they appear to denote the appropriate class of objects, although the objects themselves might have been conceived of in a different way. Since the children did not actually have the objects to refer to, their failure to overextend was inferred from their answers to the probe questions. For this reason, the comparison to Clark's work is more of an analogy than a direct correspondence. In the case of the development of ontological knowledge, some predicates could be applied sensibly to a larger class of terms, whereas in Clark's case some terms denoted a larger class of objects.

Carey (1978) has argued that an explanation for the development of word meaning by addition or subtraction of discrete features is insufficient. In some cases abstract features such as "vertical direction" do not seem to be initially acquired as components of the words such as "tall" and "short." Whereas the feature defining polarity, such as "tall" = + spatial property and "short" = − spatial property, often seems to be acquired early, a general abstract dimension of comparison is not. Thus, young children appear to learn "tall" as referring to the positive polarity of a specific spatial extent, or perhaps a spatial configuration such as narrowness, for a specific type of object. "Tall" for a building may mean large extent from ground to roof, while "tall" for a person may mean large extent from head to toe. Children may also use such vague dimensions of comparison as general size when they use "tall" with other objects such as a loaf of bread. So, instead of applying the abstract features for vertical spatial extent to all physical objects when using "tall," children appear to use "tall" in a manner that is idiosyncratic for certain types of objects.

In light of Carey's work, features should not always be viewed as discrete entities that are acquired in a unitary fashion. Instead, many features may be initially acquired in an idiosyncratic manner where their meaning varies from object to object, such as roof to street versus head to toes. Gradually over the course of development a more overarching and abstract commonality is discovered, such as vertical direction. How does this view of the acquisition of semantic features relate to the account of the growth of ontological categories? Does it mean that children use a predicate such as "is tall" in a completely idiosyncratic way with every object they encounter? If so, would that result in a haphazard tree structure that frequently violates the M constraint? It would if the immature lexical items were being used in a completely haphazard manner. However, in addition to these variable properties, there are systematic properties underlying all uses of "tall," and these systematic properties preserve the M-constrained tree structure.

Although a child may use "tall" to refer to "+ head to toe extent" for humans and "+ roof to street extent" for houses and "general + extent" for balls, in all cases the child is using the notion "positive spatial property." Thus, common to all uses of "tall" is a feature or features corresponding to the notion "positive spatial property." The differences reside in the particular spatial properties that are used for each object. It is apparent from the ontological tree that predicates with the feature "spatial property" would apply to all and only those physical objects that have boundaries. Moreover, no categories are distinguished on the basis of particular kinds of spatial properties. Thus, spatial predicates such as "tall" would cause no problems for the tree structure even though in certain respects they might have idiosyncratic uses with various object types. In fact, those aspects of a word's meaning that do not vary across objects might actually be used as data for constructing tree representations.

There are theories and studies not only on general patterns of the semantic development of lexical items but also on the development of specific types of lexical items that appear to be relevant to ontological categories. The findings on one class of lexical items, spatial terms, relate specifically to the ontological tree. One of the more interesting connections is through the work of H. Clark (1973), which deals with spatial and temporal predicates. Clark offers an ingenious account of how, during the course of development, certain spatial terms become extended metaphorically into the temporal domain. Examples of such terms include "long/short," "far/near," and other words that describe one-dimensional extent, as well as prepositions such as "at" and "between." Of the human conceptions of spatial and temporal extent that Clark posits in order to show how time can be described with spatial metaphor, the one most directly related to ontological categories is that children must first learn the meaning and use of spatial terms in the physical domain before being able to extend them to time.

The relation of these findings to the ontological tree is apparent: just as children at first use terms such as "long" only in the spatial sense, so also children at first appear to think of all terms as denoting only physical objects. The tree differentiation patterns indicate that some categories develop out of others; in particular, events seem to develop out of physical objects. Clark's theory describes a similar process. The relation between the two theories shows up in the interchange in the second grade-school study where a child is beginning to distinguish the temporal and spatial aspects of "long." This child's tree also suggests a beginning awareness of the ontological category of events.

Clark's theory has been questioned by Friedman and Seely (1976), who studied whether preschoolers acquire "after," "first," "last," "ahead of," "behind," and "together with" in the spatial sense before the temporal sense. They found no support for such a progression, as approximately half the words were used and comprehended first in the temporal sense. However, their study too may have problems with regard to selection of particular words. Although one should probably select words that have approximately equally good usage in the temporal and spatial senses like "long" and "short," their words seem to have highly preferential uses in one domain or the other; "before" and "after," for example, are much more commonly used in the temporal sense. In addition, their claims, as well as Clark's, concern the ability to comprehend terms when used in either the spatial or temporal sense, an ability that is quite a bit simpler than that of being aware of the distinction between events and physical objects and knowing the characteristic properties of each. For this reason, term comprehension and awareness of ontological categories may not be so closely related. It nevertheless appears that children are at least partially able to understand some of the terms that refer to events before they know what sorts of things events are.

Hierarchical Organization of Word Meaning

Besides the semantic work on individual lexical items, there is important and potentially relevant work on how relations between words develop. In particular, a number of investigators have been concerned with the hierarchical organization of word meanings and how this organization relates to conceptual development. However, as in the case of the research on adult semantic memory, the hierarchies are based on truth values and not sense. Nelson (1977) argues that children initially, at ages two to five, map lexical items directly onto concepts but are not aware of how such items interrelate; later, at ages five to seven, they relate words in a variety of ways ranging from functional relations to contextual relations to hierarchical relations. Finally, at ages seven on, they learn to relate semantic items mostly in terms of hierarchies. Nelson also argues that, as development proceeds, the semantic system becomes increasingly independent of the underlying conceptual system.

It is difficult to know how to relate these claims to the results of the four developmental studies because the hierarchical structures involved are different. There is, however, reason to believe that Nelson's results might not be the best indicators of how truth-dependent hierarchies develop, because most of her evidence for the so-called fundamental change in the organization of words from children to adults comes from an analysis of the literature on word association tasks, or the syntagmatic-paradigmatic shift, and from an examination of the kinds of definitions children give. There is independent evidence that the abilities underlying such tasks may not be directly related to semantic relations in the lexicon. Cramer (1974), for example, has found that while kindergartners produced mostly functional or syntagmatic responses in a free association task, they nevertheless showed more false recognitions of items that were hierarchical coordinates. Mansfield (1977), using a false recognition technique, also argues that the psychological mechanisms underlying free association responses are very different from those involved in encoding and organizing semantic memory. The same sorts of arguments seem to apply to children's definitions.

Others have claimed that children are basically unaware of the complex hierarchical relations between words until some time after age six (Anglin, 1970; Bruner, 1966; Francis, 1972; Riegel, 1970). But it appears that these investigators have been looking at abilities that, while related to lexical items, are not the basis for their semantic organization. Anglin, for example, has studied children's clustering of various items in free recall and their groupings of individual objects according to similarity. He claims that, early on, children organize objects according to highly concrete distinctions and only later do they use more abstract distinctions. Younger children do not appear to classify according to abstract concepts, such as "alive," and instead use more concrete distinctions, such as "human" versus "nonhuman." Only after age thirteen do they supposedly use the more abstract distinctions. The results of the four developmental studies are in contradiction to such a claim. The probable reason for the difference is that Anglin's tasks are measuring not only the child's semantic competence but also certain classification skills.

Besides the Mansfield study, other studies support the claim that even preschoolers are aware of some hierarchical relations between concepts. Harris (1975) discovered that four-year-olds were able to infer the qualities that an object designated by a nonsense word should have after being told that the nonsense word was the same sort of thing as a man, a bird, or a flower. The children's responses strongly suggest hierarchical organization of both semantic attributes and the words themselves. Similarly, Steinberg and Anderson (1975) demonstrated that when children were given retrieval cues to recall a previously pictured object, the probabilities of a cue aiding recall were accurately predicted from a representation of the retrieval cues in a hierarchical structure. It seems, therefore, that given the appropriate techniques, quite young children at least four years old are capable of organizing and interrelating their concepts in hierarchical arrays. This is a desirable result, since even the youngest children in the preliminary developmental study exhibited some degree of hierarchical organization.

In sum, the literature on semantic development has generally been in accordance with the findings of the four developmental studies. But it is also clear that the theory of ontological types is sufficiently different from any prior research so that most comparisons have to be indirect and inferential. The theory is able to encompass a wide variety of issues that have not been looked at in much detail in the past. It is fundamentally concerned with a structural description of how semantic concepts can be combined. This is a new emphasis, as most prior research has examined either the development of meaning of a given lexical item or occasionally the meanings of highly interrelated sets of items (Haviland and Clark, 1974). In contrast, in the case of ontological knowledge, relations between a wide variety of items are explored.

A second feature of this approach is that the theory makes a strong claim about the relations between semantic and conceptual development. Semantic phenomena such as anomaly and copredication are direct consequences of how ontological categories are organized. The predicability tree is isomorphic to the underlying ontological tree.

The theory of the development of ontological knowledge is also different from prior work in the breadth of its applicability. By arguing that certain parts of semantic and conceptual development are closely related, it presents the possibility of describing, with one device, not only how several different semantic phenomena develop but also how a wide variety of cognitive phenomena develop.

Realism

The tree theory and the results of the four developmental studies may be related to Piaget's (1929) discussion of realism. Realism, as Piaget defines it, "consists simply in situating (in) things characteristics which belong in truth to mind, but which the mind does not yet realize as belonging to it (names for example)." This so-called "primary indissociation" is contrasted to "secondary indissociation," "which consists in attributing to things characteristics similar to those which the mind attributes to itself such as consciousness, will, etc." (p.

237). The latter case is meant to explain animism. Piaget presents numerous examples of realism, such as children attributing to thoughts and dreams the properties of the things thought or dreamt about. Perhaps the most famous type of realism is nominal realism, where the names of objects are considered just as much a part of a physical object as is some other property, such as color; thus words are seen as physical, nonarbitrary properties. Vygotsky (1965) makes similar claims.

Markman (1976) has argued that it is not correct to claim that young children are true nominal realists. After all, she points out, children react very differently to the word "tiger" in a discussion and to actual tigers. Children in fact have great difficulty with intangible things such as words, and this difficulty contributes to their failure to separate the empirical from the linguisitic aspects of questions such as "Is the word 'skyscraper' tall?" Markman supports her thesis by showing that children are not "pictorial realists"; that is, they do not attribute to pictures the properties of the objects pictured. The reason, she argues, is that pictures are more concrete than words.

The results of the developmental studies suggest a new way to account for realism. Realism may just be part of a larger developmental phenomenon that is also compatible with Markman's observations. The phenomenon is that of ontological categories developing out of other ontological categories. It has been shown that some five-year-olds apparently think that all things are types of physical objects and therefore find it perfectly appropriate for physical object predicates to span events and abstract objects. This finding does not necessarily mean that ideas and dreams must have the properties of the things thought or dreamt about, but only that children attribute to them some physical properties and have great difficulty thinking of them as nonphysical entities. This interpretation is compatible with Markman's claim. Nonetheless, since children are forced to make such abstract entities physical, it is not surprising that one of their strategies is to give abstract things the properties of the physical objects that those abstract things denote. The point is that there are many other possible strategies that children can use, and they are not bound to make an entity such as a dream physical by attributing to it the properties of the dreamed-of object. Some children in the preschool study made dreams physical by thinking of them as rocks, while others thought of them as clouds, and in neither case were the dreams about rocks or clouds.

A consequence of this treatment of realism is the view that

realism is just part of a more general developmental pattern of applying to objects in category A the predicates of another category B out of which category A develops. Realism is the case where all things take predicates for physical objects. But there are also cases where all animals take human predicates; and later on, after Piagetian realism has been outgrown, there will still be an incorrect use of event predicates with abstract things. For example, an idea might be called an hour long. Thus realism can be viewed as a subphenomenon within the broader context of the theory of the development of ontological knowledge.

Metaskills

The interpretation of realism as a subphenomenon of ontological development suggests a way of accounting for how various metacognitive abilities develop. Metacognition is the ability to step back and look at various cognitive skills in themselves. In several different types of tasks younger children fail because they are unable to examine the cognitive prerequisites for success on the task. Thus, younger children fare much more poorly on memory tasks because they are apparently unable to look at memory as an entity and be aware of its limitations (Flavell, 1970). A consequence of this inability to look at memory itself is a failure to see the need for and devise more efficient memory strategies. Children who have poor intuitions about memory capacity, or about the difficulty of the material to be remembered, may not be aware of the need for efficient strategies; and although they may be able to use such strategies to great advantage when told to, they may not use them spontaneously. Similarly, younger children appear to fail on certain attention tasks because of an inability to look at attention itself. Yet a third example of metacognition is in the domain of language, where the development of the ability to evaluate tautologies is dependent on the ability to look at language and not through it. Osherson and Markman (1974) argue that the child's difficulty with both tautologies and nominal realism may be a special case of a general inability to examine objectively the abstract thing called language.

While these three metacognitive abilities—memory, attention, and language—are investigated most often, similar developmental patterns must accompany any task that requires the child to look at the cognitive skill itself. A possible explanation for this general developmental pattern is found in ontological development. Younger children do not seem to have a clear notion of a category or categories that correspond to abstract objects, and the members of such categories tend to be imbued with the qualities of physical objects, or perhaps of events. Given such difficulty conceiving of abstract entities, these children not surprisingly might have difficulty with entities such as memory, attention, and sentences. Moreover, the ages involved are generally consistent with expectations based on the results of the four developmental studies. Thus, children usually start to devise strategies in memory tasks, for example, at about the second-grade level (Flavell, 1970). At this point children also usually begin to isolate abstract objects as a separate ontological category. In sum, much of the difficulty that younger children experience in certain metacognitive tasks may be a consequence of their not yet having developed a sufficiently sophisticated awareness of abstract objects.

Causality

Children's knowledge of ontological categories also influences their explanations of causal relations. A predicability tree places constraints on the class of possible empirical laws of the form $(\forall x)\ (Px \to Qx)$; it in fact constrains virtually all expressions employing the standard logical connectives. In particular, the predicates P and Q must not be on different branches of the predicability tree. The domain of discourse for the variable x also must be restricted to just those instantiations that are spanned by both P and Q. This means that individuals with different ontological trees should have different sets of possible empirical laws.

Since the developmental results indicate that young children have different trees from adults, they should also use a different set of empirical laws in their causal explanations. More precisely, as children's trees have fewer branches and fewer spanning restrictions, children should use a larger set of laws than adults. For example, children who did not distinguish animals from plants should also be willing to state laws such as "The plant wilted because it was sorry." To use another example, children who failed to distinguish events from physical objects might claim that a recess was dirty because it happened in the mud. Adults would not make such a claim since "happens in the mud" and "is dirty" are on different branches in the adult tree.

It seems, therefore, that the tree theory makes it possible to predict precisely one way in which children's causal explanations might differ from those of adults. Of course, as in the case of natural concepts, the tree theory places only partial constraints on what constitute humanly possible empirical laws. There are undoubtedly several other reasons why a physical law might not be natural. For example, it may be self-contradictory.

These predictions about children's causal explanations are substantially different from those made by Piaget (1930) and Laurendeau and Pinard (1962). The Piagetians argue that young children do not grasp the idea of cause and effect and instead tend to relate causal phenomena on the basis of spatial and temporal contiguity. Such claims have been questioned. Huang (1943) argued that with the proper techniques, quite young children are capable of giving cause-and-effect, albeit naive explanations of various physical phenomena.

More recently, Berzonsky (1971) has shown that young children, while giving precausal explanations of remote events such as the phases of the moon, give truly causal explanations of familiar events. Similarly, Koslowski (1978) has shown that for relatively simple events, such as a concealed rod ringing a bell in a box, children infer an unseen causal mediator. Gelman (1978) also reviews several recent studies which suggest some knowledge of causal relations by young children. The theory of ontological knowledge does not make any predictions about whether given children think in a causal or precausal manner; it predicts only that, if they do, they are limited to a certain set of empirical laws.

Animism

One aspect of what has been called precausal thinking is the use of animism by the child. Piaget has given countless examples of cases where children appear to apply human and animal predicates to inanimate objects. Moons are aware of their own motion; tables feel it when they are broken; the sun sees. Perhaps the most common examples of this phenomenon are cases where children apparently think that inanimate objects such as guns and ovens "are alive" (Piaget, 1929).

The claim that young children have difficulty with the adult distinction between living and nonliving things appears to be at odds with the findings of the four developmental studies. The distinction between living things and other things is one of the strongest in the tree and was made by a majority of children even in the preschool study. Some children would think of plants as nonliving, but it was rare for a child to think that an animal predicate spanned things such as cars, chairs, and rocks.

It is difficult to know how to resolve this conflict between reports of childhood animism and the patterns of ontological development. While a number of investigators have questioned Piaget's interpretations (Huang, 1943; Klingberg, 1957; Margand, 1977), there nonetheless can be little doubt that, in the appropriate experimental paradigm, children agree that things such as the sun, the moon, and the wind are "alive." Laurendeau and Pinard, for example, conclusively documented that children agree that various inanimate objects are "alive." Thus, the phenomenon exists; the question remains whether it means that children who are animistic in the Piagetian sense do not make a conceptual distinction between animals and certain nonliving things.

An analysis of the conceptual causes of animistic responses has been made by Carey (forthcoming). She concludes that, under careful questioning, children as old as six or seven will argue that certain objects such as the sun are "alive." Moreover such responses are not limited to the predicate "alive"; other properties, such as "has bones" and "eats," are also ascribed to inanimate objects. Six-year-olds will not necessarily do this for a large number of different inanimate objects; but at least for a few objects, such as the sun, many children agree that it is alive and has some of the properties of animals.

These findings do not mean that children have no awareness of the category of animals. Although they may not have the complete adult concept, they do seem to be aware that an animal is a different kind of thing from other objects. One indication of this awareness comes from Carey's own work in which the predicates "die" and "grow" were applied to either animals alone or to both plants and animals. Carey makes an additional claim that relates directly to the ontological tree. While she might agree that children younger than six can think of plants and animals as distinct and self-contained categories, she is not of the opinion that these children have an awareness of the superordinate category of living things. She feels that this is a complicated concept requiring a good deal of theoretical knowledge about plants and animals, knowledge that a six-year-old is unlikely to have. So, even in cases where children use "dead," and occasionally "alive," with plants and animals and nothing else, Carey believes that such a common usage does not necessarily mean that those children have the superordinate concept of living things. Instead, they might be using two different senses of "dead" for plants and animals. Carey is currently conducting research that will determine whether she is correct.

It is possible that the younger children who participated in the four developmental studies did not have the concept of living things and that ambiguities inherent in "alive" and "dead" were responsible for the apparent common node between plants and animals. Some support for this view may be implicit in the Puerto Rican study, where a large number of the younger children did not have trees with such a common node since "vivo" spanned only animals. In fact, the unusual developmental pattern of first-graders committing more "errors" with "vivo" than either kindergartners or third-graders is easily explained if one assumes Carey's viewpoint. At this point the correct interpretation is not certain—whether the younger children have a common superordinate node for living things or whether both plants and animals are directly dominated by the node for bounded physical objects. Future work with several predicates and terms and the relevant nodes will be necessary before the issue can be conclusively decided.

Even in the Laurendeau and Pinard work, which is often cited as the best evidence for childhood animism, there is an indication that children conceive of plants and animals as separate categories. Thus, while children did say that many inanimate things were alive when asked "Is x alive," the same children were first asked to "Give me the names of some things that are alive." Children would often list several things, but fifteen out of fifteen things listed by various children were either a plant or an animal. This finding suggests that, at the very least, children tend to distinguish plants and animals from other things in spontaneous lists of living things. Since these numbers are based on an analysis of just those few conversations of children that Laurendeau and Pinard chose to present as examples, it is not possible to be sure that their data as a whole would show the same result; nonetheless the data available provide intriguing evidence for the children's making the distinction.

In sum, the phenomenon of childhood animism turns out to be extremely complex and not simply artifactual. Despite apparent contradictions between the work on animism and the four developmental studies, a more careful analysis reveals no real discordance.

Classification

There is a temptation to relate the theory of ontological knowledge to the development of classification skills. Much of Piaget's work on classification is concerned with how the child develops increasingly sophisticated ways of hierarchically organizing classes of objects (Inhelder and Piaget, 1964). The relation of the four developmental studies to traditional classificational studies is, however, more indirect than might at first seem. The reason—just as in the case of comparing them to studies on semantic memory—is that the predicability trees are set up according to sense, while classification trees are set up according to truth values and often cover categories all of which are part of the same ontological category.

Despite the differences between the trees used in classification research and the predicability tree, the ontological studies can still be related to some of the more general claims that have emerged from the classification literature. Piaget claims that classification develops in three stages, represented by cases where the intensions fail to define the extensions; cases where objects are organized in hierarchies but class-inclusion relations are not observed; and cases where true classification is seen (Inhelder and Piaget, 1964). The first stage is supposed to occur roughly between two and five years, the second stage roughly between five and seven years, and the last stage after seven years. This sequence would imply that many of the children at age five should be unable to form hierarchies and use class-inclusion relations. Such a prediction appears to be at odds with the fact that five-year-olds and even preschoolers honor the M constraint. If children honor the M constraint, then their ontological knowledge must be organized according to a rigid hierarchy with the standard subset-superset relations. Does this not mean that such children have classification skills?

The resolution of this apparent contradiction may lie in distinguishing conscious application of classification principles from knowledge that implicitly embodies such principles. Children who have a hierarchically organized body of knowledge are not necessarily able to make judgments about class-inclusion relations. Thus, even though children's responses result in a tree where a node for animal predicates is dominated by a node for physical-object predicates, it does not automatically follow that they would then know that there are necessarily more physical objects than animals. The judgment appears to require some degree of "meta-awareness" of classes themselves and their properties. The case may be analogous to the developmental lag between the honoring of grammatical rules in production and the generation of accurate intuitions about the same grammatical rules.

The evidence that children use class-inclusion relations even at an implicit level is controversial. In various semantic memory tasks Harris (1975), using an inference technique, Steinberg and Anderson (1975), using cued recall techniques, and Mansfield (1977), using a false-recognition technique, all concluded that the child's semantic knowledge was organized in a manner that reflected superordinate-subordinate relations. Steinberg, Anderson, and Harris go on to argue that children as young as five years appear to use class-inclusion relations.

There are problems with these studies, however. In the Harris task, for example, children did not honor the asymmetric properties of the class-inclusion relation. That is, while they did infer from a statement like "a tib is a robin" that it was a bird, had wings, and was alive, they also made the mistake of inferring from "a gug is a bird" that it was a robin.

The Steinberg and Anderson study has come under fire from Heidenheimer (1978), who argues that they confounded coordinate and superordinate relations with exemplar and action relations. She claims that, when these relations are explored independently, children's false recognitions appear to be caused by an encoding of semantic information in terms of exemplar and action relations and not in terms of the superordinate class-inclusion relation. It is not clear, however, that Heidenheimer's criticisms are completely valid. For one reason, much of her argument rests on word association data, and there appear to be problems with this method, which make it impossible to conclude from the semantic memory research that children have a complete knowledge of class-inclusion principles. There nonetheless seem to be strong indications of some degree of hierarchical organization. Future studies are needed to determine whether the organization is sophisticated enough to embody class-inclusion principles.

Other studies on classification suggest that even preschoolers have considerably more skill in classification tasks than was previously thought. Two studies in particular give indications of classification skills in certain specialized domains. Rosch et al. (1976) show that, at the so-called "basic level" of abstraction, children of all ages are able to sort objects into appropriate categories. The results of Markman and Siebert (1976) are even more pertinent. These authors draw a distinction between true classes, whose members have no interrelations, and collections, whose members have conventional interrelations, as in the case a group of people versus a family. That is, collections have an internal structure among members while classes do not. The finding of interest is that pre-schoolers who fail on standard class-inclusion problems, such as "Are there more blue blocks or blocks?" will nonetheless succeed if the class is made into a collection, as in "Are there more blue blocks or more in the pile of blocks?" Both of these studies suggest that, in the appropriate domain where classes are highly concrete and internally structured rather than arbitrary, children appear to have some knowledge of class-inclusion relations.

These examples by no means exhaust the literature concerning class-inclusion knowledge in young children. At the very least it would seem, there are important components of the knowledge of class-inclusion relations in children as young as preschoolers. What is not known is the nature of these components and how sophisticated a body of knowledge they form as a whole. The four developmental studies are compatible with the assessment that young children have, at some level, knowledge of superordinate-subordinate relations.

Of the many truth-dependent trees that accurately classify various aspects of the world, certain ones are analogous to the predicability tree. They are analogous in that they demarcate the same ontological categories (Fig. 33). It would be interesting to compare the developmental courses of the predicability tree with a typical truth-dependent analogue. Would the two trees develop simultaneously? That is, if children realize that a flower cannot be sorry, do they also realize that it is a plant and not an animal? This task is very different from the presumably more difficult standard-classification task of making judg-

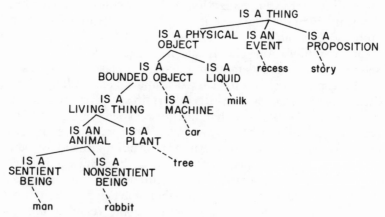

Figure 33. *Truth-dependent analogue to predicability tree*

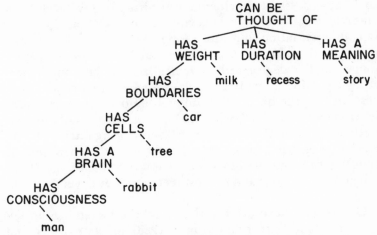

Figure 34. *Truth-dependent tree based on distinctive properties*

ments about class-inclusion relations, such as "Are there more plants or more physical objects?" It would also be interesting to compare the developmental course of the truth-dependent analogue with the development of other nonanalogous truth-dependent trees. Would the relations represented by the analogue tree have a special kind of salience? Would its developmental patterns be different?

A slightly different kind of truth-dependent tree analogue could be based on distinctive properties, or even various combinations of them, rather than on category names (Fig. 34). Again the question arises as to how such a tree develops in comparison to the predicability tree. In both types of analogues, there is an additional developmental question: if children know that an object is spanned by predicates at level x, do they also know that the object must have all properties that are at nodes dominating x? That is, if children know that something can be sorry and honest, do they also know that it must have mass and color and be a physical object?

Studies are currently under way that may provide answers to these questions. At their conclusion it may become clearer how truth-functional hierarchies and sense hierarchies are related, and how both of these hierarchies are related to classification skills.

Hierarchical Tree Structures

Historically, developmental psychologists have shown a strong interest in hierarchical structures. Werner (1940) argued that the process of development at virtually any level, from embryological to high level cognition, consisted of "concomitant differentiation and integration." Younger children's actions and thoughts are less differentiated because they have a much smaller degree of hierarchicalization. The ontological studies provide a highly specific example of this general process. In fact, the hierarchical differentiation of tree structures is strongly constrained, with only certain patterns of differentiation occurring. The relations to Werner's arguments should not be exaggerated, however, as his theory is so general that it is difficult to compare in any detailed way to the theory of ontological knowledge and the results of the four developmental studies.

Others who have dealt with the role of hierarchies in development are Bruner and Bruner (1968), Sinclair (1971), and Riegel (1970). For the most part, the relation of their views to the theory of ontological knowledge is tangential. Some work by Greenfield and Schneider (1977), however, is potentially relevant. They sought to study the development of tree representations in a domain other than language by investigating the development of children's ability to copy a physical tree structure, that is, a mobile made out of plastic straws. They found that, from age three on, there is a "systematic growth in the representation of hierarchical complexity." That is, younger children constructed only partial copies of the tree model and seemed unable to construct the entire representation with all its embeddings.

One possibly relevant aspect of the Greenfield and Schneider study is that, while young children frequently made mistakes in their copying, they rarely made the mistake of constructing a structure with downward converging nodes, that is, an M or W structure. In fact, there were no such errors from age five onward.

Greenfield and Schneider interpret their findings as supporting the hypothesis that there is "a level of cognitive organization common to language and action." They argue that the same structural features, such as interruption of constituents, which cause difficulties in language also cause difficulty in physical tree construction tasks. Thus, they claim, both action and language development are constrained by the development of a general ability to deal with hierarchical tree structures.

It would be tempting to use the Greenfield and Schneider study as support for the theory of ontological knowledge, because the patterns of increasing hierarchical complexity and lack of downward convergence are similar across the two domains. However, it is improbable that there is a general hierarchical skill underlying development in such different areas as syntactical knowledge, construction of mobiles, and ontological knowledge. General and all-encompassing principles, while appealing in their parsimony, usually break down when applied in sufficient detail to any one example. For one thing, the time courses in language and mobile construction are not compatible. A four-year-old child might easily produce a ten-word utterance that would be characterized by a well-articulated phrase structure tree with sixteen different nodes and dominance relations as deep as five links; yet the same child would not be able to produce a mobile at anywhere near the same level of sophistication. Even if Greenfield's definition of hierarchicalization in language involves embedded clauses and not phrase structures, there is no explanation why the latter do not qualify as forms of hierarchical knowledge.

An additional indication that structural properties of language and other domains, while superficially similar, arise from different underlying cognitive skills comes from a study of mine on the development of children's abilities to perceive ambiguities, both structural and "lexical," in language and pictorial displays (Keil, in press). The results show that the two abilities are uncorrelated and in fact have very different developmental patterns. Thus, while the Greenfield and Schneider work is compatible with the development of ontological categories, it is not at all clear that the similarity is more than superficial.

In summary a wide range of developmental literature is relevant to the development of ontological knowledge. The literature confirms two major points. First, the theory of ontological knowledge and its development may be applied to a wide variety of developmental phenomena ranging from anomaly intuitions to causal thinking. Moreover, the theory offers a new unified perspective from which to view many of these phenomena. This appears to be the case, for example, with Piagetian realisms. Second, by and large the developmental literature is compatible with the developmental data gathered in the four studies. The few apparent incompatibilities resolve themselves on closer examination of the actual experimental settings.

9 | A Closer Look at the Theory

THERE CAN NOW BE no question that the theory of ontological knowledge offers a coherent account of the knowledge underlying and responsible for a number of different psychological phenomena. Most important, it has been shown, at least for the predicates and terms investigated, how the M constraint is a strong organizing principle that governs not only the structure of adult knowledge but also the development of knowledge. In addition, the tree representations that are constructed on the basis of the theory afford a new perspective on semantic and conceptual development, making it possible to see certain powerful developmental patterns for the first time. Thus, at least for the domains investigated so far, the theory has explanatory psychological value.

There remain, however, two types of questions concerning the theory itself. The first involves the nature of the tree representation. Are there any M-constraint violations inherent in the tree as it now stands, and are any such violations caused by natural extensions of the tree structure? The second type concerns other problems with the tree structure or extensions of it. For example, are there legitimate arguments for eliminating pseudo M and W structures, such as distinguishing literal from metaphorical usage?

Downward Tree Proliferation

The term "category mistakes" is preferable to "selection restrictions" because not all forms of lexical incompatibility are represented in the tree. This distinction is important since, without it, nothing prevents the tree from branching endlessly downward. For example, if every predicate-term incompatibility is to be represented in the tree, there will have to be a different branch for every animal that makes a characteristic sound.

After all, only turkeys gobble, only dogs bark, only cats mew, only cows moo, and only horses neigh. There would probably be at least fifty branches required just in the area of animals and their sounds.

Both Smart (1953) and Cross (1959) have pointed out this problem in critiques of Ryle's (1938) original description of category mistakes. Smart argues that for almost any category, one can discover anomalies that would, by Ryle's account, force the breaking up of that category. An example of such an anomaly would be, "The seat of the bed was hard," which would force chairs and beds into different categories. Smart then points out that this is absurd since certainly the class of all furniture should be a single category. Cross makes essentially the same arguments and offers several other examples of distinctions that split up coherent categories, which he uses as evidence against the whole classical notion of categories.

If the only problem were one of too many branches, or distinctions, the solution would be simple. One could declare that toward the bottom of the tree the anomalies gradually become weaker and that the anomalies higher up on the tree are the more interesting. Correspondingly, as the sentences become less and less anomalous, they will increasingly appear to have a truth value, most likely false. The argument would be that the theory is correct no matter how many distinctions are drawn; it is just that the only ontologically interesting ones are near the top of the tree. The fact that there would not be any exact level at which the anomalies suddenly failed to become category mistakes would not in itself be troubling.

There is, however, reason to believe that if trees did proliferate downward, the theory would not be correct and several M-constraint violations would arise. To use a particularly vexing example, "is pregnant" and "is impotent" might be said to span just females and just males, respectively. This would suggest the following tree fragment:

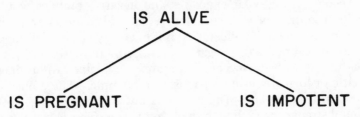

IS ALIVE

IS PREGNANT   IS IMPOTENT

The problem arises when predicates such as "is sorry" are now considered. It is evident that not all pregnant or impotent things can be sorry; for this reason, "is sorry" would have to be located below both of these predicates in the tree. The only way to do this without violating the M constraint is to make "is sorry" ambiguous with a meaning different for males than for females. This is clearly not a welcome result as no one wants to claim that men and women must be sorry in fundamentally different ways. Adherents to Sommers' theory are therefore motivated to come up with a reason for excluding sentences such as "The man was pregnant" and "The mouse neighed" as true category mistakes.

There are several related ways to deal with this problem. Probably the simplest is to argue that sentences such as "The mouse neighed" are not anomalous at all but simply false. Of course, this solution requires that true category mistakes not be false. It also means we have to develop a way of distinguishing false from anomalous sentences. One approach would be to use the procedure employed in the developmental study and see if the sentences are still anomalous when negated. This will help to dispel many problem sentences, but not all, for a number of reasons.

First, even if the "not" is adjacent to the predicate, it is sometimes difficult to be sure of its scope, that is, to know whether the whole sentence or just the predicate is being denied. The sentence "The idea is not green" could be interpreted as "The idea is not able to be green" or "The idea is some other color." Under the first interpretation, "The idea is not green" would have a truth value, while in the second case, it would be a category mistake. Therefore, even if a subject did state that "The idea is not green" was sensible, the subject might nevertheless think that "The green idea" was a category mistake. Some have taken the view that the negations of category mistakes must always be true (e.g. Ewing, 1937), while others have argued that such negations must be meaningless (e.g. Pap, 1960). Each may be right depending on the scope of the negation operator.

Second, using polar opposites and negative prefixes would help to control the scope problem but would create a new problem in that many predicates do not have any clear polar opposites and cannot take a negative prefix. And third, sometimes a sentence may be unacceptable because it violates various pragmatic or logical presuppositions. For example, "The mouse is 1000 miles tall" and "The mouse is not 1000 miles tall" both sound strange, even though the latter is true. This is because it would be bizarre for a person to utter either statement. In the case of logical presupposition, it may be argued that both "The present King of France is bald" and "The present King of France is not bald" sound strange even though neither is a category mistake. Whether presuppositions are to be characterized in this manner is controversial, but regardless of precise characterization, the problem of unacceptability caused by factors other than category mistakes remains.

Since the negation strategy does not eliminate all undesirable sentences, another technique is needed. One approach would be to appeal to a different set of intuitions, namely those of judging whether a predicate-term combination is in any way conceivable. If a person can conceive of a situation in which a sentence could have a truth value, then that sentence is not a category mistake. This device works quite well with "The mouse neighed." It is quite possible to conceive of a mouse neighing, while it does not seem possible to think of an argument being green without changing "argument" or "green" into a different lexical item. One can also test for conceivability by asking, "How could you tell if x was P?" It is obvious how to tell if a mouse had neighed, but it is quite another matter to think of any way of telling whether a rock was honest.

The general idea of drawing the distinction between category mistakes and other anomalies by appealing to the conceivability of the statement has been proposed in different forms. Cornman (1968) proposes that true category mistakes are only those sentences that a normal perceiver could not perceive as being true. Similarly, Sayward and Voss (1972) argue that if a sentence could at any time be true about an object, then that sentence can never be considered a category mistake. For example, one can imagine a time at which "The seat of the bed was hard" could be true. This, therefore, is an argument against Smart's (1953) objection. Sayward and Voss claim that Strawson (1970) makes a similar distinction between category mistakes and other anomalies when he argues that belonging to a category is a property that covers an object's whole temporal span, if it has one.

Harrison (1965) proposes a somewhat different way of making the distinction. He argues that categories are language-neutral and that any correct translation of a category mistake remains a category mistake. By contrast, "mistakes of usage," such as "The seat of the bed was hard," may be correctly translated into an expression that is not a category mistake. Thus, one can imagine a language in a country where all beds have seats. Harrison proposes that the real mechanism behind category mistakes involves various naming devices that enable

humans to apply names to things. Each device can apply only
to a certain class of things, and such a class is an ontological
category. A device is supposedly limited in its application because of the nature of various physical conditions in the world.
"If no physical conditions of this general sort existed (that is, if
there were no possibility of dividing time by reference to some
regular notion of periodicity) then the . . . day of the week device would cease to have any point" (p. 321).

The four developmental studies refute this suggestion by
demonstrating that the same physical world does not force different organisms, such as adults versus children, to have the
same categories. Categories are in the head, not in the world.

It might be argued that the whole notion of conceivability is
inappropriate. Does it make any sense even to talk about impossible concepts and unthinkability? If not, then conceivability could not be used as a diagnostic tool for isolating category
mistakes. A different argument is that conceivability is a sensible notion but still too crude a measure for distinguishing category mistakes. Thus a 22-sided polygon might be inconceivable since one cannot think of it as distinct from a 23- or
21-sided one. Nonetheless, a 22-sided polygon is clearly not a
category mistake. Such criticisms seem misdirected. Conceivability is a workable notion once its various senses are clarified. Drange (1966) deals with these criticisms in considerable
depth and marshals strong arguments for the usefulness of conceivability.

One possible problem with the conceivability strategy is
that it may not work as well in the case of "pregnant men."
Some find it quite easy to conceive of a man being pregnant,
but others claim that to do so, one has to change the meaning
of "pregnant" or "man" in an essential way. Apparently, the
conceivability criterion is not sufficient for everyone.

Another possible way to distinguish the case of "pregnant
men" from that of "tall ideas" is to use the notions of logical
versus categorical impossibility. "The man is pregnant" is logically impossible, while "The idea is tall" is categorically impossible. This difference implies in turn that "The man is
without child" is a tautology, while "The idea is short" is still
a category mistake. One possible reason for this difference is
that the contradiction in the case of "pregnant men" is at a different level of meaning than the contradiction for "tall ideas."
"The man is pregnant" seems to involve a contradiction at the
level of definitions, as in "The bachelor is married." "The idea

is tall" seems to involve a contradiction at a much deeper level having to do with the incompatibility of two categories. The distinction between a definitional level of meaning and a deeper level gains support from the observation that definitions of terms almost always make distinctions among members of the same ontological category. For example, a "butcher" is defined as someone who cuts meat, not as a human, an animal, or a physical object.

Contradictions such as "The man is pregnant" and the "The bachelor is married" are called "logical" because it is believed that a detailed analysis of the lexical entries for "man" and "pregnant," or for "bachelor" and "married," would reveal a logical contradiction where both P and not P would be asserted about the object. By contrast, no logical contradiction could be derived from the lexicon for "The idea is green."

Drange (1966) has independently chosen a similar path in an attempt to distinguish category mistakes, or as he calls them "type crossings," from contradictions. Drange draws the distinction by first defining three kinds of sentences: those that are "logical truths" which "can be proved by appeals to rules of logic alone," those that are "simple definitional truths" which "can be converted into a logical truth by substituting for (one or more) terms in a sentence the conventional definitions of those terms," and those that are "definitional truths" which are either simple or "follow logically from some set of simple definitional truths" (p. 28). As examples of sentences of each type, Drange offers "All male parents are parents" as a logical truth, "All fathers are parents" as a simple definitional truth, and "All fathers have children" as a nonsimple definitional truth, namely one that follows logically from "All fathers are parents" and "All parents have children."

Given these definitions, Drange argues that contradictions are "definitional falsehoods" and consist of "the negation of a definitional truth." Because they are negations of definitional truths, it is possible to convert them into logical contradictions simply by substituting for the relevant lexical items their conventional definitions. By contrast, Drange argues, type crossings, or category mistakes, are not self-contradictory and a logical contradiction cannot be derived by substituting definitions for terms. Drange believes that category mistakes are also falsehoods but of a different type from definitional falsehoods. He argues that category mistakes are synthetic a-priori falsehoods. However, the fact that Drange thinks category mistakes to be false and not meaningless does not weaken the point that category mistakes seem to be distinguishable from self-contradictions on the basis of a definitional account.

Sommers (1963) himself makes a distinction between contradictions and category mistakes but does not refer to definitions. Instead he discusses how incorrect sentences can be incorrect at different levels of rectitude. Englebretsen (1971) explores Sommers' notion of levels of rectitude in more detail and formulates an order of four levels from "lowest" to "highest": ungrammatical, category mistaken, logically inconsistent, and empirically false. A sentence can be defective at any one of these levels. In addition there is an interdependency between the status of a sentence at two different levels such that, if a sentence is either correct or incorrect at the highest level, it must be correct at all levels. Thus the empirically false, or incorrect, sentence "The Eiffel tower is red" is logically consistent, not category mistaken, and is grammatical. Conversely, if a sentence is incorrect at a low level, it is inapplicable at higher levels. Thus, while a category mistake is grammatical, since grammaticality is at a lower level than category mistakeness, it cannot even be evaluated at the higher levels of logical consistency and empirical falsehood.

In sum, both Sommers and Englebretsen distinguish category mistakes from self-contradictions via the notion of levels of rectitude. As Englebretsen puts it, "We have, then, a clear way of distinguishing between things like red numbers, square circles, and faster than light dog sleds" (p. 68). Englebretsen gives other arguments in support of these distinctions and also attempts to relate them to different types of possibility.

One question remains. If category mistakes are not consequences of contradictions in definitions, what are they consequences of? One possible resolution is to say that there is a contradiction in what is presupposed rather than in what is defined. This approach would depend on the view taken of the presuppositional nature of a language, but at least one such view is compatible with such a view of category mistakes. Allwood, Andersson, and Dahl (1977) consider, in addition to logical presuppositions, three types of presuppositions that occur in natural language: existential, factive, and categorical.

Sentences with existential presuppositions presuppose the existence of some entity. For example, the sentence "Jimmy's mom is remarkable" presupposes that Jimmy has a mom. Sentences with factive presuppositions presuppose certain propositions as facts. Thus, the sentence "It is strange that Bruce always wears a white coat" presupposes that Bruce always wears a white coat. Finally, sentences with categorical or sortal presuppositions presuppose certain domains of discourse. As Allwood et al. put it, "a sentence $F(a)$ presupposes that a is in the domain of F." Thus $F(b)$, where b is a term that is not a member of the set a, will have no truth value and will be meaningless. McCawley (1968) also characterizes the difference between anomaly and contradiction by arguing that the former is a contradiction in presuppositions.

Thus, category mistakes may be a result of violations of a certain type of presuppositions while self-contradictions are not. The precise nature of the violation of the presupposition is not important at this point. It may be that one could derive logical contradictions by comparing the presuppositions of the predicate and the term in a category mistake. Or the nature of the violation may be considerably more intricate. Such issues must await further analysis of both presupposition and category mistakes. So far there is at least one coherent account of presuppositions that captures the distinction between self-contradictions and category mistakes.

In sum, the issue of downward tree proliferation is not troublesome for Sommers' theory. There appear to be a wide variety of different ways to draw a distinction between category mistakes and other kinds of incompatibilities. Moreover, this distinction has been drawn by several different investigators. While the skeptical reader may not find any one argument completely convincing, the weight of all of them together is highly persuasive. There are also very few troublesome cases such as "The man is pregnant." In most cases, such as "The mouse neighed" and "The idea is green," it is quite clear what type of incompatibility is involved.

Possible M-Constraint Violations

Certain terms and predicates high up in the general predicability tree appear to violate the M constraint. Are they all ambiguous? There may be some problematic cases.

The first problem is that some predicates seem to violate the M constraint but do not seem to be ambiguous. One example is the predicate "clever." One can have a clever man and a clever idea yet the word "clever" does not seem to be obviously ambiguous here. Careful examination of how "clever" is used suggests a solution to this dilemma. When used with men, "clever" appears to mean "has a lot of intelligence, is quick witted, is mentally able." None of these definitions are appropriate for "clever" when used with ideas. Why, then, does "clever" not seem ambiguous?

The answer may be that it is not just a coincidence that ideas and men are described by the same phonological shape, but rather that one sense of "clever" is derived from and closely related to the other. When an idea is clever, "clever" means something like "is the kind of thing thought of by a man when he is being clever." A zeugma shows how two different senses of "clever" are involved: "The man was not very clever today, but the idea was."

This same phenomenon can be seen with certain terms, such as "fire" and "song." A fire can be red and an hour long, and a song can be an hour long and about pollution. What reason is there to believe that these terms are ambiguous? Probably the strongest argument comes simply from careful reflection. When a fire is red, one is talking about the flames; when it is an hour long, one is talking about the action of burning. Similarly, a song is an hour long in the singing and about something because of its content.

One might object that in the case of fires, books, and the like the zeugma test fails and that such terms are therefore not ambiguous. When a term is truly ambiguous and the ambiguous alternatives are in different categories, perhaps the result should always be a zeugma, as in "The bat was hungry and was a Louisville slugger." Certainly the sentence "The book is heavy and is about birds" is a good deal more acceptable than the sentence with the word "bat." But this does not mean that "book" is not really ambiguous as an abstract entity and a physical object.

Sommers (1965, 1971) discusses such potentially problematic terms explicitly. He considers, for example, the phrase "Italy is sunny and democratic" and the fact that it does not form a zeugma. It fails to be zeugmatic, Sommers argues, because people tend to form by convention certain category hybrids when two entities are regularly and closely associated. Thus societies and geographical places are commonly associated with each other and a category hybrid is then formed. Sommers states that there are certain "heterotypical entities" which are experienced and which suggest hybrid categories. The same phenomenon is exhibited when one says the fire was red and happened yesterday. The event (the action of burning) and the physical object (the flame) are intimately associated with each other, and therefore a hybrid category is formed. Sommers stresses, however, that these hybrid categories are not violations of the M constraint because the user is aware of the hybrid nature.

It therefore seems that some terms, such as "fire," "book," and "Italy," are not simple lexical ambiguities, like "bat," "book," and "tank." They represent a special case in which entities are intimately related in the world and may even appear to be a single object but in fact have dual ontologies. The ambiguity seems to be in the object itself rather than simply in the term. A sunny, democratic Italy refers to a hybrid category, but that category itself is ambiguous. As Sommers (1971) states, "What we refer to is a category composite, a heterotypical entity composed of things of different types" (p. 27). Kripke (1978) also argues for the notion of certain objects having dual ontologies.

The Italy that is sunny and democratic is not an individual but rather a heterotypical entity if the M constraint is to hold. Sommers (1965) offers a criterion by which to determine if a given entity is an individual. An entity spanned by predicates P and Q is an individual if and only if there are no things that are spanned by P and not Q and no things that are spanned by Q and not P. Thus a brief red fire is not an individual since recesses can be brief but not red and fire hydrants can be red but not brief. This criterion, while helpful for pointing out the difference between individuals and heterotypical entities, cannot be taken as support for the M constraint since it essentially presupposes it. It basically states that an entity is not an individual if it creates a violation of the M constraint.

Since Sommers' criterion cannot be used to provide support for the M constraint, it is desirable to have a test which objectively demonstrates whether cases such as "heavy, romantic books" and "brief, red fires" are heterotypical entities, and which does not presuppose the M constraint. One possible test is to try to make precise paraphrases that can take only one of the two predicates. Thus "The fire was red" can be accurately paraphrased as "The flames were red," but "The flames were an hour long" is a category mistake. "The song was an hour long" can be paraphrased as "The singing of the song was an hour long," but "The singing of the song was about pollution" is anomalous. This test would be effective to the extent that the paraphrases are considered accurate. If intuitions about paraphrase accuracy are reliable, then the two senses of the terms should be apparent. There is also the requirement that in nonambiguous cases, no paraphrase should produce an anomaly, although at present there is no way to prove that it cannot.

The paraphrase test does not presuppose the M constraint and appears to be able to handle all heterotypical entities by showing that there is a subtle kind of ambiguity inherent in the terms that refer to such entities. While the test assumes that individuals can have reliable intuitions about what constitute accurate paraphrases, such an assumption does not seem to be problematic. Gleitman and Gleitman (1970), among others, have shown that such intuitions are usually quite accessible to subjects.

There is another instance where a true violation of the M constraint may be found in the predicability tree. Such an instance involves terms such as "tall" and "heavy." In Figure 1 "heavy" dominates "tall" since milk can be heavy but not tall. This relation holds because all aggregates and fluids without obvious boundaries do not seem to be able to take spatial predicates. There does exist, however, a certain class of entities that appears to be spanned by spatial predicates but not by predicates such as "heavy." Perhaps the best example of such an entity is a hole. A hole can be skinny and tall but certainly not heavy or light. Holes, therefore, appear to create a violation of the M constraint, as do two-dimensional entities.

There does not seem to be any easy way to resolve this violation. One possible solution would be to claim that "The water is tall" is not a category mistake but rather a different kind of predicate-term incompatibility. One could then argue that "tall" and other spatial predicates dominate predicates such as "heavy." While it seems that the anomaly found in "tall water" is not as strong as other category mistakes, such an explanation is ill advised. As yet, there is no justification for arguing that mass noun-spatial predicate combinations such as "The water is tall" are not category mistakes. There also do not seem to be any ambiguities in the predicates "tall" and "heavy" or in the term "hole" that would allow breaking up the M constraint.

It therefore seems at this point that two-dimensional things, or conversely mass nouns, might create a true violation of the M constraint. If this turns out to be the case, the result would not be problematic. The fact remains that, even if this violation is real, the M constraint is still an extremely powerful principle that governs the vast majority of predicates and terms. In fact, this conception is consistent with the finding that children have great difficulty in learning the full adult meanings of spatial terms such as "tall" (Carey, 1978). That is, if the M constraint is a strong cognitive principle in development, it should be difficult for children to learn the meaning of a term that violates that constraint; and such is the case with most spatial terms.

This argument is analogous to common arguments in linguistic theory in cases where violations of a syntactic constraint are difficult for children to learn. For example, C. Chomsky (1969) has demonstarted that not until ages eight or nine are children able to comprehend sentences that violate the syntactic "minimal distance principle."

In sum, most apparent violations of the M constraint are just that, apparent and not real. Careful reflection, zeugmas, and the paraphrase test usually reveal some lexical ambiguity or occasionally a deeper type of ambiguity in the entity denoted. However, there may still be genuine violations associated with mass nouns, nouns denoting two-dimensional terms, and spatial predicates.

It may be possible through future work to resolve this dilemma by means of a more precise characterization of the role that mass nouns play in the theory. At this time, however, no straightforward solution presents itself. But even if the problem turns out to be real, it could not be serious because the violations would be limited to just one small part of the tree, while most predicates and terms would still honor the M constraint. There are other ways that M structures can be generated. For example, violations of syntactic aspect frames, such as, "He received the letter for three hours," might also create M structures. Such violations, however, do not seem to be the same as category mistakes and thus are probably not creating M structures in the predicability tree.

Contextual Influences

Another problem deals with those predicates and terms whose meanings seem to be especially dependent on their sentential contexts. Consider, for example, the predicate "good." Some might argue that ideas are "good" and knives are "good" in very different senses of the word. In fact, virtually every term in the tree might be seen as good in a different way. Should "good" be put at the top node of the tree as one predicate, or is it ambiguous in n ways for n nodes? Putting it at the top node has intuitive appeal, but then one must justify doing so with "good" while still asserting that "clever" is ambiguous. Is there really any difference in the way that sense varies for "good" versus "clever"? It may not be possible to use the paraphrase test to resolve this issue since the paraphrase of "good" when used with "knife" might not be applicable to "idea" unless it is in the most general form. It is also not completely satisfying to claim that context-sensitive predicates are special cases that should be excluded from the tree, especially since it can be argued that all predicates are somewhat influenced by context. But the idea of setting aside predicates such as "good" as special may have merit if it is considered in a slightly different way.

Certain logical connectives, such as "and" and "or," have been called syncategorimatic, the idea of being that their meanings are completely defined by the ways they are used in various logical arguments. Perhaps words such as "good" should be considered syncategorimatic. It would then seem less ad hoc to exlude "good" from the theory since its meaning would be of a special type. Keenan (1979) has argued that "in general transitive verbs are interpreted as functions on their objects and exactly how a transitive verb is interpreted varies with the choice of object." Thus, Keenan claims, "cut" is the same verb in "cut the class" and "cut the cake" and the difference in meaning is a function of the two objects. If Keenan is correct, then a large number of predicates such as "cut" would either end up at the top node of the tree or would be excluded as syncategorimatic, neither of which would be a welcome result for the theory of predicability and ontology. It seems, however, that while the two cases of "cut" may have some similarities in meaning, they are definitely ambiguous and are not analogous to "good."

n-Place Predicates

Thus far, the theory of predicability and ontological knowledge has been limited to one-place predicates. It is not difficult, however, to extend it to predicates that take any number of terms as arguments. The method of extension is illustrated by the example "x hates y." This predicate fits into the tree in two places: when x is held constant and when y is held constant. In the first case, the intuitions are about what sorts of things could be hated. Since it seems that anything can be hated, "x hates—" would be put at the top node of the tree. In the second case, the intuitions are about what sorts of things can hate; and here, "—hates y" would probably be put at the same node as either "is sorry" or "is hungry."

This technique assumes that there is an additional constraint on the theory: no matter what the category of the term x which is being held constant, the resultant predicate, such as "*x* hates—" will span exactly the same objects. To illustrate with a different example, consider the predicate "*x* ate *y*." The *x*'s seem to be humans and animals while the *y*'s seem to be physical objects with boundaries. The claim is that "(humans) ate—" and "(animals) ate—" span exactly the same class of things. Conversely, both "—ate (plants)" and "—ate (animals)" should span identical classes of things. There are no obvious counterexamples to this constraint.

One final example shows how complex this technique for handling *n*-place predicates can become. Consider the three-place predicate "*x* is between *y* and *z*." At first it seems that *x*, *y*, and *z* are all simply at the level of physical objects. Then one realizes that a recess can be between lunch and art class. Since, however, a recess cannot be between lunch and New York City, it must then be concluded that "between" is ambiguous and that in one case *x*, *y*, and *z* are limited to physical objects while in the other case *x*, *y*, and *z* are limited to events.

Classes Without Unique Predicates

Fjeld (1974) has claimed that since Sommers' tree seems to contain classes without unique predicates, his whole proposal is doomed. Fjeld points out that it is essential to Sommers' proposal that every individual belong to a type. He then argues that if a class of terms does not have a unique predicate, such as nonhuman animals, then it is not a true type: "Now whatever can be significantly said of all non-human animals can also be significantly said of persons. That is, whatever spans all non-human animals also spans persons. So the set of non-human animals does not constitute a category" (p. 413).

Sayward (1976), in replying to Fjeld's objection, appears to commit a mistake himself by confusing falsehood with anomaly. Nevertheless the Fjeld objection is not much of a problem, for one can simply say that the class of nonhuman animals is clearly and uniquely defined as the class spanned by "is asleep" but not by "is sorry." Perhaps Fjeld's problem is that he is taking the tree as representing a purely linguistic phenomenon and not also as an underlying conceptual framework.

Distinguishing Metaphorical and Literal Meaning

The simplest argument that there is a distinction between metaphorical and literal usage lies in the use of words "metaphorical" and "literal." The phrase "literally speaking" is usually well understood, and virtually any adult can perceive certain sentences either literally or metaphorically, depending on instructions. The question then arises as to whether an independent measure can be used to decide the unclear cases. If this turns out to be impossible, it will not destroy the theory; one does not have to resolve all fuzzy instances for a distinction to be valid.

One independent measure would be the paraphrase criterion that was suggested for ambiguities. Take, for example, the metaphor "John killed the idea." One paraphrase of "kill" would be "to cause *x* to cease its life function forever." This paraphrase would be anomalous if combined with "idea." The criterion would be that if at least one paraphrase of a predicate produced an anomaly with a term, then that predicate-term combination would be metaphorical or elliptical. This criterion raises the question of what an acceptable paraphrase consists of, but that question at least seems to require a different and more readily available intuition (cf. Gleitman and Gleitman, 1970). One possible problem with this solution is that even if no paraphrase that creates an anomaly is found, one cannot be completely sure that the expression is literal; a more thorough search might uncover such a paraphrase. There does not seem to be any way that one could prove that an anomaly-creating paraphrase did not exist.

Modal Notions

The predicability tree may represent two different necessity relations. These are of interest not only for their own sake but also for possibly providing yet another way of distinguishing between category mistakes and other sorts of predicate-term incompatibilities. The first necessity relation is directly related to the idea of a category mistake. An expression that is a category mistake is necessarily not true. But it is not also necessarily false, as category mistakes differ from contradictions which do seem to be necessarily false. In fact, it is probably the case that category mistakes are necessarily neither true nor false. As a result, sentences must be able to be assigned values other than true and false, or strings without such values must not be considered sentences. This proposal may be more intuitively appealing if it is stated in terms of possibility: "It is not possible for a category mistake to be true nor is it possible for it to be false." This proposal helps to determine if certain strings are true category mistakes. For example, it seems wrong to state that it is necessarily the case that mice do not neigh. It also seems wrong to claim that it is necessarily the case that men cannot be pregnant.

A different and perhaps more interesting necessity relation is a consequence of the tree structure. It is necessarily the case that for all x, if x is a human, then x is also an animal, a living thing, and a physical object; or in a slightly different form, it is necessarily the case that for all x, if x is honest, then x is possibly hungry, alive, tall, and heavy. Here "x is possibly hungry" is equivalent to stating that "x is hungry" is sensible. The fact is that the predicability tree seems to represent a great number of necessary truths, perhaps all those in the domain called "conceptual necessity."

It seems reasonable to propose that there are four kinds of necessity that can figure into the following expression: $L(x)(Px \to Qx)$, where L means "necessarily" and "(x)" means "for all x." These are logical necessity, mathematical necessity, physical necessity, and conceptual necessity.

It may be argued that ultimately conceptual necessity will have to soften into "conceptual connectedness," because nothing is inconceivable given time and additional subject matter. Support for this view reportedly comes from the history of science, where notions that were supposedly inconceivable at one time are now considered commonplace. In accord with this view Sommers (1971) argues that only the M constraint is constant and that particular tree configurations and categories may change dramatically as scientific knowledge progresses. But the trees may not be that plastic, and any truly inconceivable notion, such as a "green idea," may never become conceivable. Humans may be constrained not only by the M constraint but also by whatever particular categories they are able to conceive. Under this circumstance, much of what appears to be a restructuring of the tree may instead be an instance of a predicate shifting its meaning in that it now occupies a new position in the same categorical structure. This is not to say that the categories are completely fixed or cannot differentiate but that there are limits on the types of changes that may occur. If the four types of necessity do exist, it seems reasonable to propose that the predicability tree represents all cases of conceptual necessity. This, if true, would demonstrate the tree's powerful contribution toward a description of natural concepts.

The necessity relation in the form $L(x)Px$ is commonly known as a *de dicto* modality because necessity is attributed to the proposition. Another more controversial necessity relation can be expressed as $(x)L\ Px$. This is a *de re* modality because necessity is attributed to the possession of a property by a thing

(Hughes and Cresswell, 1968). Despite its controversiality (Quine, 1953; Kripke, 1972), modality *de re* may be closer to what the tree embodies. The tree seems to represent the fact not that certain propositions must be true but rather that, if an object has property P_1, it must also have properties $P_1 \ldots P_n$. After all, if the tree is supposed to be a structural ontology, it should be about things, not propositions.

These four types of necessity are similar to distinctions proposed by Englebretsen (1971). Englebretsen argues that there are three types of possibility: empirical, by which he means physical possibility; logical, by which he means both arithmetic and logical possibility; and categorical, which appears to be analogous to conceptual possibility. These three types of possibility are meant to be comparable to the three levels of rectitude of empirical falsehood, logical inconsistency, and category mistakes. Englebretsen further claims that these levels of possibility are ordered as follows: if something is empirically possible, it must also be logically possible and categorically possible; and if something is logically possible, it must also be categorically possible.

If these different types of necessity are legitimate, they lead to an important developmental question. Do children learn all types of necessity at roughly the same time, or is there some invariant order of acquisition of the various types? The data suggest that not all types of necessity are understood at the same time. The fact that even the five-year-olds had intuitions that generated M-constrained trees suggests that they have the notion of conceptual or categorical necessity. Yet there is evidence that children of this age are unable to understand logical necessity (Osherson and Markman, 1975). It may be that those types of necessity which are embedded in concrete examples, such as conceptual necessity, are easier to learn than those types that depend on a more abstract set of rules, such as logical necessity. This difference appears to be analogous to Markman and Siebert's (1976) observation that nonarbitrary classifications, or collections, are easier to learn than arbitrary ones.

The entire discussion of necessity and ontology should, however, be viewed with caution. For example, Kripke (1972) has demonstrated that the relations between conceivability and necessity are not as straightforward as previously thought.

Other Ontological Systems

Several others besides Sommers and Ryle have argued for high-level categories that seem to be of the same sort as those demarcated by intuitions about category mistakes. Frege (1950) defines categories by using the notion of criteria of identity. He argues that there are different criteria of identity for all different categories of things. Thus the criteria used in deciding on the identity of two physical objects are different from those used in deciding whether two events are identical. Stevenson (1976) points out that Frege does not give a "criterion of identity for criteria of identity." That is, it is not known when the criteria are different or the same. Quine, for example, argues that in principle there is no reason why events and physical objects could not really be one huge category of four-dimensional things. Despite this problem, and despite a discomfort with the distinction between necessarily false propositions and meaningless ones, Stevenson remains convinced that there are high-level categories of the type Sommers suggests.

A different method for discovering ontological categories has been proposed by Caton (1971). Caton argues that for a given simple sentence, there are certain *wh*-questions that "essentially arise" out of that sentence. A question is essentially arising if it is not possible to give the answer "no-*C*" where *C* is the questioned constituent. For example, given the sentence "John went to Petaluma," one can ask, "When did John go to Petaluma?" Such a question must be answered with reference to a time; assuming the truth of the original sentence, one cannot reply, "At no time did John go to Petaluma." But if asked the nonessentially arising question "Who did John go to Petaluma with," it is possible to reply "No one."

Caton argues that these questioned constituents in essentially arising questions can be regarded as important in fixing the ontological categories inherent in a language. These constituents can also be replaced by indefinite pronouns to make a sentence that is entailed by the one originally questioned. Thus, "John went to Boston sometime" is entailed by "John went to Boston"; while "John went to Boston with someone" is not entailed. Caton claims that "there is a kind of minimal set of things, linguistically speaking, that figure in phrases of the form '*wh*-*C*' in questions that essentially arise, in indefinite pronominal phrases, and in universally negativized constituents . . . An important reason . . . for regarding this minimal set . . . as, in part at least, determining the ontology inherent in a natural language is that . . . this set of things is related, via essentially arising questions, to the truth or falsity of the simplest statements that can be made in the language" (pp. 34–35).

While Caton does not go into detail as to what ontological categories are discovered through such a means, he at one point mentions that all the concepts of a person, of being alive, and of being in a certain place at a certain time are discoverable by this procedure. Moreover, he argues, those questions that essentially arise from a sentence are intimately related to the presuppositional structure of that sentence. The types of categories Caton suggests as well as the connection to presuppositions bear a strong similarity to features of Sommers' ontological program.

Another approach to an ontology has been made by Katz (1966, 1972). Indeed, Caton himself refers to Katz's theory of redundancy rules as a related method for discovering ontological categories. Katz (1966) points out that Aristotle's basic categories, while intuitively appealing, are not justified by any explanation of why or how those particular categories are arrived at. Katz argues that, within the context of a theory of language, one can discover basic ontological categories quite similar to those proposed by Aristotle. In particular, a certain part of Katz's theory of language, namely the structure of lexcial readings, reveals not only basic categories but also their interrelations. Katz and Fodor (1963) propose that a lexical item contains a list of semantic markers with a different marker for each conceptual component of the meaning of that lexical item. But this proposal in itself is inefficient since a large degree of redundancy would be present in most lexical readings. Thus the semantic markers "physical object" and "animal" would appear as entries in all readings for any word denoting an animal. Moreover, while any reading with "animal" would also have "physical object," the converse would not hold, since the reading for "chair," for example, would not include the marker "animal." Relations such as these have led Katz to propose that certain "redundancy rules" are part of a person's knowledge. The redundancy rules are of the form "Animal" → "physical object" and allow a person to have a lexical reading with just "animal" as an explicit marker and to recover other markers such as "physical object" via redundancy rules.

Katz never gives a complete set of redundancy rules but lists examples of the kinds of markers that would enter into redundancy rules. They most frequently include "human," "plant," "animal," "artifact," and "physical object." The ontological tree captures all the redundancy rules between these entities, if upward-pointing arrows are simply added to all links. This does not mean that the ontological tree is isomorphic to the complete set of redundancy rules of a language as put forth by Katz, for while Katz on occasion discusses the hierarchical nature of redundancy rules, some of the markers entering into his redundancy rules, such as "vehicle," are below the level of the categories in the predicability tree and would probably casue M violations. Katz also appears to believe that the redundancy rules terminate at levels such as "physical object" or "event," and consequently no rules are present to join these high-level nodes together to form one unified hierarchy. Instead, one would have several fragments without the uppermost links. Despite these differences, the parallels between the ontological tree and Katz's system of redundancy rules are striking. It might well be possible to modify the redundancy rules in such a way that they would be captured by the full tree structure and at the same time not do serious harm to Katz's theory.

Katz considers the truly basic ontological categories to be only those semantic markers that are implied by other markers but which do not imply other markers themselves, namely the top nodes in the fragments. In fact, he explicitly discusses how the categories inherent in Ryle's category mistakes are much less abstract than the ones he proposes and are of a different type. These terminal categories should perhaps not be given such a special status. One reason for such a status would be that they are the uppermost nodes in the redundancy rule fragments, but if redundancy rules prove to be modifiable so that they fit into the tree, then these categories would no longer have a special status since only the single top node representing "all things" would be an upward terminal node.

There are too many possible ontological systems proposing categories similar to those generated by a theory of predicability to explore them in detail. The point they lead to is that Sommers' theory of predicability is more than likely just one facet of an extremely basic part of human knowledge. By uncovering other facets, such as identity criteria, essential arising questions, and redundancy rules, one might be able to gain a more thorough understanding of that knowledge and its many ramifications. While the knowledge certainly seems to be a representation of what sorts of things there are, namely an ontology, only by considering its many manifestations can one really understand what that means.

The literature on ontological categories reveals that philosophers of many different persuasions seem to agree on the existence of certain basic distinctions and categories. It is interesting to see to what extent these general categories can be

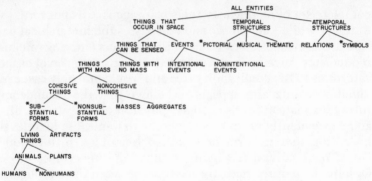

Figure 35. *General ontological tree (asterisks denote categories without unique English predicates)*

represented in the predicability tree, if its nodes are labeled by category names with various philosophical origins (Fig. 35). When compared to the predicability tree (Fig. 1), some new distinctions emerge and a few old ones change, but more important, many of the categories do fit into the tree and do not violate the M constraint.

Not all "philosophically basic" categories are directly represented by predicates at a given node. A node could exist but have no simple English predicates that distinguish it on the basis of sense. For example, there is a class of objects that are "substantial," meaning that each of their parts is not just a smaller instance of the whole. If you cut a tiger in half, you do not get two tigers; but if you cut a rock in half, you get two rocks (ignoring cases involving size where a rock could become two pebbles). Such a class of objects does have a node in the tree, but it is not clear whether there are any predicates that cluster at this node.

It is therefore necessary, not that any basic category have a predicate node in the tree, but rather that a node be constructed for this category in such a way that it does not create an M or a W. This law is yet another indication that the "real" tree is a nonlinguistic structure upon which language is incompletely overlaid.

The part of the tree representing abstract entities is not as well differentiated as that for physical objects. This is not surprising in that there has not been much philosophical agreement on what distinctions should be made in this area. A few of the more likely ones are shown.

The Predicability Tree and Conceptual Knowledge

Sommers' tree theory is more than just a theory about natural language. It is related to underlying conceptual knowledge. Both Sommers and Englebretsen (1971) insist that categories demarcated linguistically by predicability are isomorphic to ontological or conceptual categories. This assertion is not completely accurate if "isomorphic" is used in the set theoretical sense. If the two trees were completely isomorphic, then every category in the ontological tree would have a counterpart in the linguistic tree. But several examples have been given of cases where ontological categories do not seem to have any specific linguistic counterparts in English.

The claim should be that every linguistic category must have a corresponding ontological category. Moreover, all ontological categories that are not expressed linguistically must nevertheless fit into the same tree with those that are; that is, they cannot create M-constraint violations. A further relation might be that all ontological categories are potential linguistic categories. To put it another way, the ontological tree is potentially isomorphic to the linguistic tree. This relation, though reasonable, is not a certainty since some nodes in the ontological tree may be inexpressible linguistically for reasons unrelated to predicability. There seems to be ample evidence that certain categories fit perfectly into the tree but are not demarcated by English predicates. Nonhuman animals is one example of such a category. Furthermore, other languages are able linguistically to represent categories that are not evident in English. For example, German marks the human/nonhuman distinction. The best way to explain these observations would seem to be that all humans tend to share the same ontological tree and, depending on their language, they express linguistically only a certain subset of all the ontological categories.

If some deeper conceptual categorization of the world is assumed to be the basis for predicability, this tells something about human cognition. The M constraint can be thought of as a necessary but not sufficient condition for a concept to be natural, provided that concepts can be defined as logical combinations of predicates. For a concept to be natural, it must be composed of predicates that denote the same category or categories that are supersets or subsets of one another. Predicates that denote categories of completely different types cannot be components of the same concept. This condition on conceptual naturalness is completely independent of content. It does not matter what each category consists of; all that matters is that predicates denoting different categories cannot be part of the same concept. This condition can be stated in a way that avoids the claim that concepts consist of logical combinations of predicates. Instead a concept can be called natural if those things that it is about form a complete ontological category. That is, a concept cannot be about things that are on different branches unless it is about all things under the lowest node dominating those branches.

There is a second, more controversial way in which the tree theory might constrain the class of natural concepts. It may be that many ontological categories are universal and are consequences of how humans conceive of the world, although this is not a claim made by Sommers. Perhaps the strongest support for this claim is that people can communicate with each other. If at least some of the major categories were not universal, then many of the statements made by others would appear to be category mistakes. This argument would be more compelling if the same trees could be generated for speakers of many different languages, providing that certain translation problems could be overcome. The Puerto Rican study provides preliminary evidence along these lines.

Sommers (1970) discusses how the advent of modern physics created a category mistake in that electrons are both waves (events) and things with mass (physical objects). He argues that this causes a radical restructuring of the tree whereby all physical objects are seen as subcategories of events. In other words, "This category organization permits talk of blue events and talk of tables as occurrences" (p. 39). Yet this restructuring may be conceptually non-natural. Even though it may be empirically true that something can be both a physical object and an event, humans may not be able to conceive of this easily if they retain their prior meanings of "physical object" and "event." Those who claim that the restructured tree is natural have probably changed the meaning of "event." Perhaps they are equating events with things that have a location in space, namely the node representing events and physical objects in the initial tree.

Even when many specific ontological categories are acknowledged to be universals, there is still a controversy over whether those universals are a consequence of the way humans structure the world or of empirical impossibility. That is, the claim is made that people cannot conceive of certain categories because they are empirically impossible. But this claim is wrong on two counts: not all empirically impossible things are category mistakes, and some category mistakes may be empirically possible.

An example of the first reason is things that travel faster than the speed of light. Such things are empirically impossible and yet are quite conceivable and certainly are not category mistakes. A large number of science fiction writers would be out of business if to exceed the speed of light constituted a category mistake. A possible example of the second reason is Sommers' electrons. Drange (1966) agrees that empirical impossibility does not result in universal category mistakes, but he nonetheless believes that there are properties of the world that dictate all category mistakes. A Martian would not, Drange argues, think that certain category mistakes were sensible. Predicate-term anomalies are like square pegs and round holes. It is not the individual who is the cause of the incompatibility, but the objects themselves. Moreover, Drange argues, if one person can conceive of a predicate-term combination while another cannot, it is not because the task is subjective or relative; rather, the situation is analogous to the case where a paralyzed person is unable to put a round peg into an appropriate hole. It is not that the relation between the peg and the hole is different for that person, but just that he or she is unable to perform the task. Whether the peg fits the hole is a purely objective matter, as are category mistakes.

Drange's claims are probably too strong. It is unlikely that all category mistakes are purely objective and that all organisms with language would come up with the same set of category mistakes. The developmental data probably cannot be used as a form of refutation, however, since Drange would most likely argue that children are analogous to the paralyzed peg-fitters. A better counterargument would be that since there are logically an indefinitely large number of different ways of categorizing the world, it is impossible that the world constrains all organisms in such a way that they can only discover certain categories. A more plausible alternative seems to be that humans have internal psychological constraints on what categories they can naturally conceive of. Both Goodman (1965) and Quine (1960) have made similar arguments with respect to the problems of induction and indeterminancy of translation.

The ontological categories are not "built in," however. Instead, all normal humans have a strong predisposition to think that there are certain sorts of things in the world. Stated in terms of Chomsky's (1975) proposal, one can investigate various cognitive domains by trying to discover the function *LT*

(Learning Theory) that maps experience into a cognitive state. In this case one wants to discover *LT(H,C)*, the learning theory that maps humans and their experience into the cognitive structure that accounts for the way they categorize the world. This cognitive structure may be defined as that which decides which concepts are natural. Chomsky avoids stating that any categories are innate; rather he maintains that, given a certain set of experiences, one can predict the mental structure that a human will have. Furthermore, over a wide range of experiences, only one small class of structures will be generated. In this sense the categories are universal; all normal humans who grow up without clearly bizarre experiences, such as brain damage, end up having mental structures that categorize the world the same way.

Such a view does not mean that there might not be differences between individuals on all categories. Rather, there are probably severe constraints on the class of ontological categories that a human can naturally discover. Thus people who disagree on the mind-body problem might have different trees since dualists could have a separate node for the "mind" which is different from the "body," but the constraints would still be tight and would not allow just any alternative. The developmental studies lend support for this claim in that the categories develop according to highly specific patterns. Children might honor the M constraint and yet have entirely different categories from adults. The main difference between children and adults is that children use a subset of the adult categories.

Two conclusions can be drawn. First, the theory of predicability, in particular the M constraint, holds up well against a number of different criticisms. Moreover, methods are developed that allow one to deal with future potentially problematic cases. There may be some violations that cannot be handled at present, but they appear to be tightly circumscribed and do not seem to constitute a major threat to the theory.

Second, the proposed theory of predicability and its relations to ontology is closely connected to a number of different topics in the philosophical literature. Perhaps the most important relation is to other theories about how to uncover ontological structure. There are striking similarities between the structures suggested by the different approaches. This resemblance offers the prospect of future work with a variety of different techniques that may all converge to yield the same structure.

10 | Constraints and Development

I T HAS BEEN SHOWN not only that the M constraint is a powerful constraint on natural concepts, but also that ontological knowledge is apparently organized in a rigid hierarchic fashion, which manifests itself in a variety of phenomena such as predicability. In addition, the M constraint is honored throughout development even though the tree representations show considerable change with increasing age. Finally, the child's knowledge, as represented by the trees, develops according to highly specific patterns. Two final questions that need to be answered are: Why do the M constraint and the specific developmental patterns exist, and how does the child make the transition from one knowledge structure to the next?

Reasons for the M Constraint

The most important element of the theory of ontological knowledge is clearly the M constraint. The question about the reason for the M constraint's existence assumes that the world itself is not organized according to a strict nonconvergent hierarchy. If the world were organized in such a fashion, it would be possible to argue that the ontological tree was merely a reflection of the world and was not a constraint on human cognition at all. Such a view seems implausible. So, let it be assumed that the M constraint is a constraint on human cognition and that there may be aspects of the world that violate the M constraint and thus are difficult to conceive of. Given these assumptions, one has to ask what purpose the M constraint serves. At first glance the constraint might seem actually to be an impediment in that it may make certain aspects of the world difficult or perhaps even impossible to conceive

165

of. One might well ask why humans should have to wear such a conceptual straightjacket. The reply to these questions is that, far from being a liability, the M constraint might well be an asset. There are at least two lines of argument for such a view, hierarchical and ontogenic.

Inasmuch as the M constraint ensures that any tree representation is a rigid hierarchy, one way to try to explain its presence is to look for general advantages offered by hierarchies. Simon's (1969) arguments about hierarchies are relevant. While he covers the advantages of hierarchical organization in functioning systems ranging from organic molecules to economic theory, he also specifically addresses the issue of the simplest type of description of complex systems. Simon argues that, where there is redundancy in the elements that make up a system, a hierarchical description of that system is likely to be considerably simpler than some sort of unstructured list of all the elements in the system. The hierarchy is a more economical form of representation because it has what Simon calls "stable subassemblies," which can be repeatedly accessed as units.

The argument that redundant information can be more parsimoniously represented in terms of hierarchical descriptions was also made by Katz (1966) when he introduced his so-called redundancy rules, which seem to be intimately related to the ontological tree. The redundancy inherent in the ontological tree is readily apparent. Any element in category A not only shares a certain set of features with all other elements of that same category but also shares the exact same features with all elements in categories that are dominated by A. Furthermore, that particular element shares some subset of these features with all elements in categories that dominate A. Thus a tiger shares the features relating to "animal" and "physical object" not only with all other nonhuman animals but also with humans. In addition, it shares the features for "physical object" with elements of higher-level categories. Given this kind of redundancy and Simon's argument, humans may well utilize a hierarchical form of representation so that they can access redundant chunks of information as single units.

This argument does not require that the world be organized in such a way that redundant elements form a strict hierarchy. Rather, it suggests that there is a good deal of redundancy and that one efficient means of representation is to use hierarchical descriptions. If this type of representation is the result of a strong bias or cognitive constraint, then those aspects of the world that violate a rigid hierarchy might be difficult to conceive of. Simon presents some compelling arguments as to why physical systems themselves are likely to evolve in such a way as to have hierarchical organization, and it may well be that these local hierarchies provided the initial impetus for the M constraint even though these hierarchies as a conglomerate exhibit all sorts of downward convergences.

At this point the argument for a cognitive advantage to hierarchic description is highly speculative. Without good accounts of redundancy, simplicity, and the like, one cannot provide strong support for such a claim. Moreover, a sophisticated account would be needed to explain why ontological categories appear to have the special status that they do. Such an account would probably revolve around the notion of ontological categories being the most "psychologically basic" categories which are presupposed by all other sorts of categorical distinctions. In addition, one would have to demonstrate why a rigid M-constraint at the truth-functional level would too severely limit the range of descriptions. There is no reason, however, why these issues cannot be clarified with future work.

Some of the more compelling reasons for the existence of the M constraint arise from a developmental perspective. One argument involves the general notion of constraints and the role they must play in the acquisition of knowledge. It seems indisputable that, at least logically, there are an indefinitely large number of different ways of conceptualizing the world. Moreover, people have been notoriously unsuccessful at finding a measure of the physical world that would predict entirely objectively which conceptualization is the "best." Almost invariably one has to revert to the claim that certain concepts are so bizzare it is silly to think that humans would spontaneously come up with them. But this sort of argument crucially presupposes the existence of a priori constraints on what are and are not natural concepts.

Given the fact that children have only a limited amount of time to develop a conceptual system which is sufficiently similar to that of other individuals so that they may communicate with them, there must be a powerful set of constraints that severely limit the sorts of hypotheses about the world that children generate. Although the M constraint is probably only a rough approximation to one of several constraints on conceptual structure, it nonetheless could certainly play a role in making the children's task easier. This argument has been made elsewhere, perhaps most forcibly by Chomsky with respect to the acquisition of language. Recent developments show that this argument can be made highly specific. Culicover and Wexler (1978) have noted that it does not seem possible to learn, in a measurable amount of time, certain aspects of syntax without a priori constraints similar to those universal constraints developed by linguists. Recently, Osherson (1978) has demonstrated that constraints also appear to be involved in natural deduction systems and in psychological models of simplicity.

A second ontogenic argument that is specifically directed to the M constraint and the ontological tree concerns the acquisition of new words. Consider children who have just heard a word for the first time, say "boojum." Moreover, assume that the children heard the word in the context of a sentence such as "The boojum is hungry." To the extent that the children have an M-constrained predicability tree, that simple phrase might actually convey a great deal of additional information for them. Suppose that the children have a simple three-node tree of the type shown in Figure 29; that is, they are aware of the three categories of inanimate physical objects, animals, and nonphysical objects. If the children were then to hear "The boojum is hungry," they would know a good deal more than the simple fact that boojums can be hungry. They would also know that boojums are animals, and that they have mass and color.

In short, the M-constrained tree allows children to make inferences about the meaning of a word given only one sentence about that word. Of course, not all predicates are equally efficacious. Thus, "The boojum is interesting" is uninformative, while "The boojum is honest" tells a great deal about other necessary qualities of boojums. Moreover, as the developmental studies have shown, children may misinterpret a predicate's meaning, in which case their inferences might be different. Miller (1978) makes a similar point in discussing how redundancy rules might help children learn the meanings of new words.

This latter fact about children's mistaken placement of predicates in the tree points to an interesting relation between the proposed involvement of the predicability tree in the acquisition of word meanings and the specific patterns observed in the four developmental studies. Consider, for example, the pattern of predicates moving down the tree with development. In the younger children's trees, a predicate might span more terms than it would in adult trees. In such a situation—for example, when "honest" spans all animals—children who hear "The boojum is honest" might infer that a boojum has the properties of animals and of higher ontological categories, but would miss the fact that boojums are sentient beings. These children would then not make any mistaken inferences about boojums but would also not make all possible ones and in effect would treat "The boojum is honest" the same as "The boojum is hungry."

By contrast, consider children who, rather than having a predicate too high, have it too low. For example, the children might believe "is alive" spans only humans. In such a case the children upon hearing "The boojum is alive," might actually make the mistaken inference that boojums must be like humans, when in fact they might only be a type of Cretan rosebush. In general, it appears that children who have predicates too high up in the tree may not extract as much information from certain sentences as they should; but those children usually make many fewer mistaken inferences than do children who have predicates that are too low in the tree.

This account is somewhat oversimplified, for the advantage of the upward-collapsed tree over the downward-collapsed tree in the learning of new words is dependent on the categories represented by the nodes involved. It also depends on whether the predicate has been moved up because its meaning is misunderstood or because the term's meaning is misunderstood. Nevertheless, it does seem from the different possible combinations that the learning of new word meanings would be more efficient with an upward-collapsed tree in which predicates move down with development rather than the opposite. Careful analysis will be necessary before this hypothesis can be verified, but in view of the purposes served by the M constraint it offers an interesting suggestion as to how the M constraint and the specific developmental patterns might be interrelated.

The same sort of arguments might also be made with regard to some other developmental patterns. Thus the fact that inversions of adjacent predicates are rarely seen may well be related to the fact that such inversions would cause all sorts of mistaken inferences about word meaning. It may also be that the pattern of terms denoting categories before their predicates is related to how word meanings are acquired, although the nature of the relation is not clear at this point. The point is not that these particular proposals are precisely correct. Nor does the manner in which words are acquired exert a major influence on the development of ontological knowledge, which would appear to be putting the cart before the horse. Rather, the point is that these suggested reasons for the M constraint are likely to yield insight into why the particular developmental patterns occur.

How Trees Develop

Even if a satisfactory answer is eventually given to why the M constraint exists and why the trees develop as they do, there still exists the question of how it is that children's knowledge increases from one tree to a larger more differentiated one. An example may help to illustrate why the problem is more than a trivial one.

Suppose that children were aware of only the categories of animals and all other physical objects and understood only predicates that applied to those two categories. How could these children learn about abstract objects? If the children could think only in terms of physical-object predicates, how could one ever explain what an idea was to them? It would be impossible to do so in terms of physical-object predicates. One could tell the children what an idea was not, but that would in no way be sufficient to convey what it was.

In general the question is how children who understand only predicates in certain categories can ever learn about a new category. In theory, the same problem could exist for adults. Imagine the difficulty in explaining or comprehending what a "ribbit" is where a ribbit is not a physical object, nor an event, nor an abstract object and has its own unique set of predicates, except for those at the top node of the tree. It is not even clear where one would start.

The most likely solution to this problem lies along the lines of a proposal that children have some rudimentary knowledge of the predicates for a new category before they actually become aware of that category as a separate ontological entity. Exactly what form this knowledge takes and how it influences the acquisition of a new categorical distinction must await future investigation. It cannot simply be the case that children must have the adult knowledge of predicates before they can distinguish a category. According to one frequent developmental pattern, terms are set aside in a separate category before they have unique predicates. Yet there are indications that quite young children have some knowledge of complicated predicates. Thus young children who cheerfully agree that a chair can happen yesterday, might also insist that their birthday party did not happen yesterday but happened the week before. In short, children appear to be able to use some predicates, but not all, in comprehension at a considerably earlier age than they realize the sorts of things to which those predicates apply. It would seem that those aspects of the predicate that are used in comprehension may also be the ones that clue children into a new ontological category.

The implications of this line of thought are provocative. If it is true that one needs some knowledge of the predicates that apply to a category in order to be able to conceive of that category, then children must have prior to the learning experience a knowledge of sets of predicates at every node in the ontological tree. This hypothesis does not lead to the conclusion that all concepts are innate, but it does suggest that there might be yet another set of powerful constraints whose function is to limit grossly the sort of predicates that children learn.

The route to an explanatorily adequate theory of natural concepts is apparently to discover constraints that delimit the class of all and only humanly natural concepts. Moreover, these constraints must play a vital role in the acquisition of conceptual knowledge. One putative constraint called the M constraint, which constrains the structure of ontological knowledge, plays an important role not only in structuring adult ontological knowledge but also in governing the development of that knowledge. Moreover, the ontological level of analysis provides a particularly illuminating perspective on various aspects of semantic and conceptual development, as well as on certain phenomena in adults. While further research may demonstrate that the theory of ontological knowledge is not completely correct, it offers a unified and coherent account of previously disparate phenomena, an account that yields new insights about natural concepts and how they develop. Any alternative theories should be able to achieve equivalent generality if they are to be successful.

Beyond the specifics of the theory, the general strategy of seeking constraints on human knowledge in any conceptual domain is a valid one. The developmental studies at least demonstrate the feasibility and the heuristic value of using such an approach to study semantic and conceptual development.

Appendixes
References
Index

Appendix A
Sommers' Proof of the Law of Categorical Inclusion

Sommers offers a proof of the law of categorical inclusion that is based on a definition and an axiom.

Definition. Two predicates P and Q are copredicable if a sentence conjoining them is about something and if that something is either one of the terms spanned by P or one of the terms spanned by Q. Stated more formally, $U(PQ) \equiv (PQ)$ is about $|P| \lor (PQ)$ is about $|Q|$, where $U(PQ)$ means that P and Q are copredicable of some term, and $|P|$ means all the terms of which either P or $-P$ is true. $|P|$ can also mean all the predicates at the same node as P.

Axiom. If a sentence (PQ) conjoining P and Q is about something, then that something is in the universe of discourse of (PQ), where the universe of discourse of (PQ) is defined as $|P| \land |Q|$. In other words, $(x)(x \in V(PQ) \equiv (x \in |P| \land |Q|))$, where $V(PQ)$ stands for the universe of discourse of (PQ).

From these assumptions, Sommers offers the following proof:

$$U(PQ) \equiv (|P| \subset V(PQ)) \lor (|Q| \subset V(PQ))$$
$$U(PQ) \equiv (|P| \subset |P| \land |Q|) \lor (|Q| \subset |P| \land |Q|)$$
$$U(PQ) \equiv (|P| \subset |Q|) \lor (|Q| \subset |P|)$$

The last line is the law of categorical inclusion. This statement of the law is ambiguous. Since P can stand for either the class of predicates or the class of terms spanned by those predicates, the law applies to both classes of terms and classes of predicates.

The proof also has drawbacks (e.g. Englebretsen, 1971). First, it depends on the reasonableness of the definition and the axiom. In particular, the notion of "about" is assumed to be straightforward. Only to the extent that it is so is the proof convincing. Second, there seems to be a flaw in the proof. Since the axiom is expressed only as a left-to-right conditional, it is difficult to see how the first line of the proof is a biconditional. Instead, it and the ensuing lines should all be left-to-right conditionals. But this would be an unwelcome result since, without the final line as a biconditional, it would be impossible to infer the relation of copredicability from the tree. The solution seems to be to strengthen the axiom to a biconditional. Such a strengthened version does not seem to be any less intuitive than the original version.

Given that the law of categorical inclusion is valid, Sommers claims that two theorems can be derived from it which illustrate more directly why the M constraint must be honored. The two theorems are:

$$U(PQ) \land U(QR) \land N(PR) \equiv (|P| \subset |Q|)(|R| \subset |Q|) \land -(|Q| \subset |P|) \land$$
$$-(|Q| \subset |R|) \land -(|P| \subset |R|) \land -(|R| \subset |P|)$$

and

$$-[U(PQ) \land U(QR) \land U(PS) \land N(PR) \land N(QS)],$$

where $N(PR)$ means that P and R are not copredicable of any term.

The gist of the first theorem is that, given the information on the left side of the biconditional alone, one knows that Q will dominate both P and R in the tree. This theorem is the basis for showing that a unique tree can be constructed from intuitions about the sensibility of certain predicate-term combinations.

The second theorem states that there can never be a certain combination of intuitions. This must be the case, for the only structure that can possibly satisfy the relations inside the brackets is of the type:

This structure, however, is a violation of the M constraint, and the second theorem states that it is not possible to have such a structure.

Appendix B
Generating an M-Constrained Matrix from Random Data

By Kevin Cotter

The probability of generating, from random data, a matrix that satisfies the M constraint is insignificant. To prove it, let E_{mn} be the event that an $m \times n$ matrix satisfies the M constraint. Further, let E^*_{mn} be the event that an $m \times n$ matrix has at least two rows that satisfy the M constraint with each of the other $m - 2$ rows (not necessarily with each other). Also let $p_{mn} = P(E_{mn})$ and $p^*_{mn} = P(E^*_{mn})$. $E_{mn} \subseteq E^*_{mn}$, so $p_{mn} \leq p^*_{mn}$.

From these one can prove the theorem:

$$p^*_{mn} = \left[\frac{3(3^n - 2^n) + 1}{2^{2n}} \right]^{2m-4}$$

The proof requires the lemma:

$$p_{2n} = \frac{3(3^n - 2^n) + 1}{2^{2n}}$$

Proof of Theorem

Let S_{mn} be the given matrix, and let $S_1, S_2 \ldots S_m$ be the rows. Let $S_i, S_j, i \neq j$, be rows that each satisfy the M constraint with each of $S_1 \ldots, S_{i-1}, S_{i+1} \ldots, S_{j-1}, S_{j+1} \ldots, S_m$. The events that S_k, $k = i, j$, satisfy the M constraint with $S_l, l \neq i, j$, are independent and each have probability $\frac{3(3^n - 2^n) + 1}{2^{2n}}$. Since there are $2(m - 2) = 2m - 4$ such events the probability $p^*_{mn} = \left[\frac{3(3^n - 2^n) + 1}{2^{2n}} \right]^{2m-4}$

As m, n increases, p^*_{mn} vanishes rapidly (Table 15).

Proof of Lemma

Define order (E_{2n}) as the number of elements in E_{2n}. Then order $(E_{2n}) = 3(3^n - 2^n) + 1$.

If the first row is empty or full, there are 2^n possible combinations of

177

Table 15 *Probabilities for various row-column combinations*

| | | | | | | | Column | | | | | |
Row	3	4	5	6	7	8	9	10	11	12	13	14
2	.9063	.7656	.6191	.4873	.3771	.2886	.2194	.1660	.1252	.09430	.07091	.05327
3	.8213	.5862	.3833	.2375	.1422	.08331	.04814	.02760	.01569	.00889	.00503	.00284
4	.6745	.3436	.1469	.05640	.02022	.00694	.00232	7.60×10^{-4}	2.46×10^{-4}	7.91×10^{-5}	2.53×10^{-5}	*
5	.5540	.2014	.05633	.01339	.00287	5.78×10^{-4}	1.12×10^{-4}	2.09×10^{-5}	*	*	*	
6	.4550	.1181	.02159	.00318	4.09×10^{-4}	4.82×10^{-5}	*	*				
7	.3737	.06921	.00828	7.55×10^{-4}	5.81×10^{-5}	*						
8	.3069	.04057	.00317	1.79×10^{-4}	*							
9	.2520	.02378	.00122	4.26×10^{-5}								
10	.2070	.01394	4.66×10^{-4}	1.01×10^{-5}								
11	.1700	.00817	1.79×10^{-4}	*								
12	.1396	.00479	6.85×10^{-5}									
13	.1147	.00281	2.63×10^{-5}									
14	.0942	.00165	1.01×10^{-5}									

* probabilities $< 10^{-5}$

the second row satisfying the M constraint since any combination works. If the first row contains k x's, let the x's be in the leftmost spaces as follows:

$$\overbrace{\qquad\qquad}^{k}\quad\overbrace{\qquad\qquad}^{n-k}$$

x x x x . . . x

If in the leftmost k spaces the second row is either empty or full, the remaining $n-k$ spaces can contain anything. Otherwise, the remaining $n-k$ spaces must be empty. Thus, given k x's in the first row, there are $2(2^{n-k}) + (2^k - 2)$ possible arrangements of the second row that satisfy the M constraint. Since there are $\binom{n}{k}$ ways the first row can have k x's, the total is:

$$2 \cdot 2^n + \sum_{k=1}^{n-1} \binom{n}{k} [2^{n-k+1} + 2^k - 2]$$

$$= 2^{n+1} + 2 \sum_{k=1}^{n-1} \binom{n}{k} 2^{n-k} + \sum_{k=1}^{n-1} \binom{n}{k} 2^k - 2 \sum_{k=1}^{n-1} \binom{n}{k}$$

By the binomial theorem,

$$\sum_{k=0}^{n} \binom{n}{k} 2^k = \sum_{k=0}^{n} \binom{n}{k} 2^k \cdot 1^{n-k} = (2 + 1)^n = 3^n$$

hence

$$\sum_{k=1}^{n-1} \binom{n}{k} 2^k = 3^n - 2^n - 1$$

Similarly,

$$\sum_{k=1}^{n-1} \binom{n}{k} 2^{n-k} = \sum_{k=1}^{n-1} \binom{n}{k} 2^k = 3^n - 2^n - 1$$

and

$$\sum_{k=1}^{n-1} \binom{n}{k} = 2^n - 1$$

Substituting into the original equation,

$$\begin{aligned}
\text{Order } (E_{2n}) &= 2^{n+1} + 2(3^n - 2^n - 1) + (3^n - 2^n - 1) - 2(2^n - 1) \\
&= 2^{n+1} + 3(3^n - 2^n - 1) - 2^{n+1} + 2 \\
&= 3(3^n - 2^n) + 1
\end{aligned}$$

Since there are 2^{2n} matrices with two rows and n columns, this gives:

$$P(E_{2n}) = \frac{\text{order } (E_{2n})}{\text{order (all matrices)}} = \frac{3(3^n - 2^n) + 1}{2^{2n}}$$

Appendix C
Three Grade-School Studies

The predicates are in upper case, and the terms are in lower case. Parentheses indicate a high degree of subject uncertainty. Asterisks designate backup predicates and terms.

First Study

Kindergartners, A1–A16

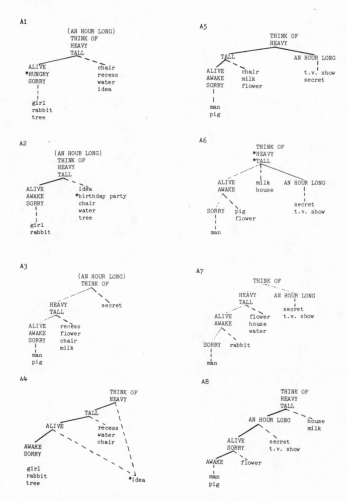

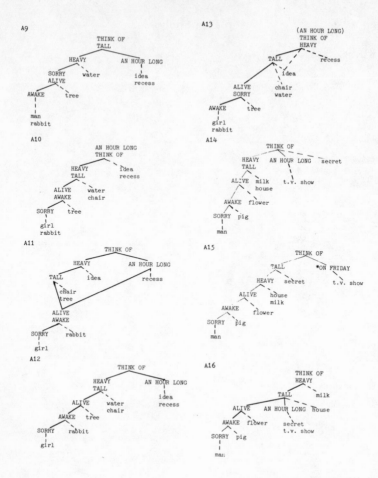

Second-Graders, A17–A32

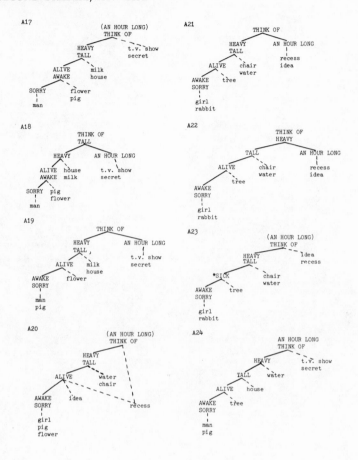

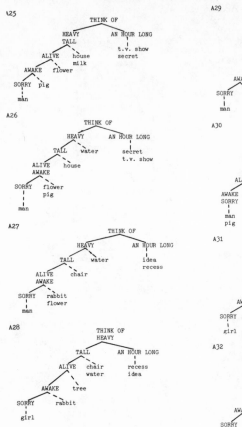

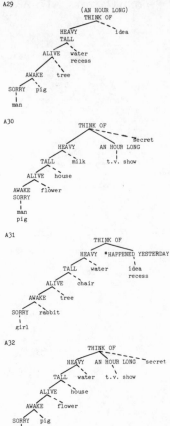

FOURTH-GRADERS, A33–A48

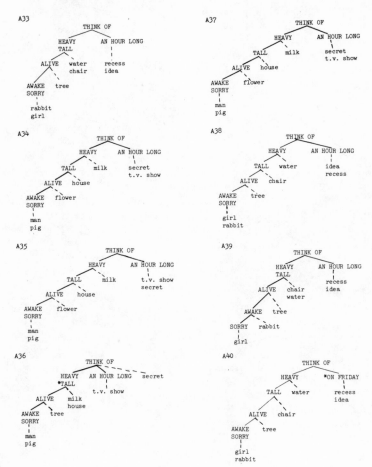

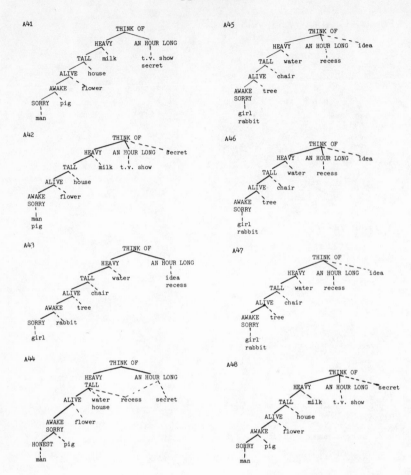

Sixth-Graders, A49–A56

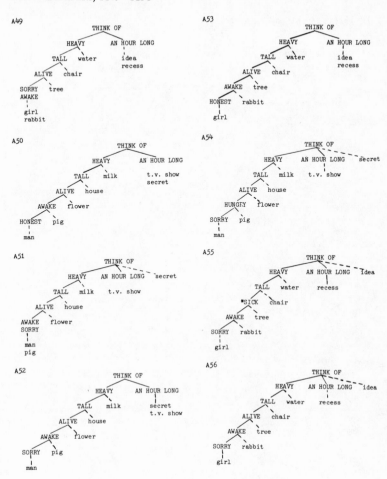

Second Study

Kindergartners, A57–A72

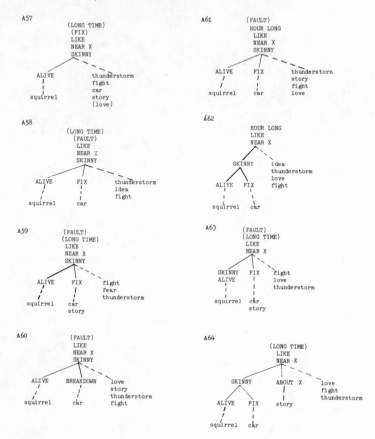

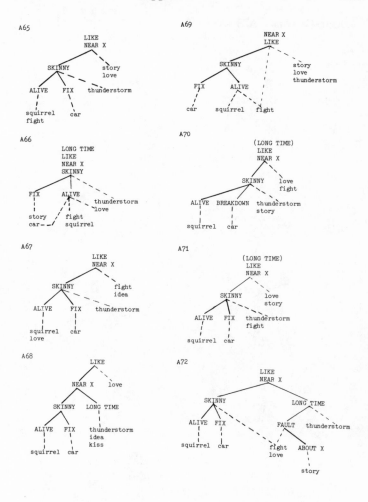

SECOND-GRADERS, A73–A88

A73
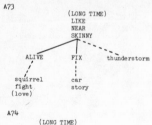

A77
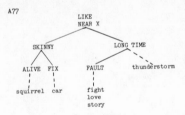

A74
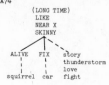

A78
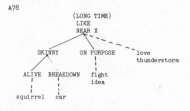

A75
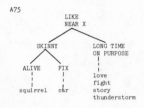

A79
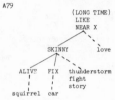

A76
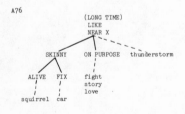

A80
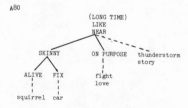

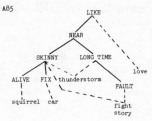

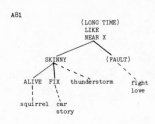

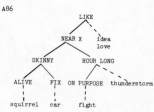

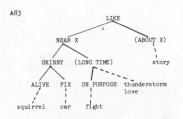

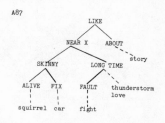

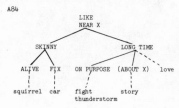

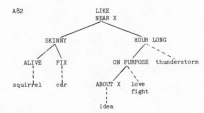

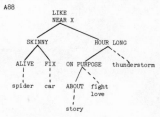

FOURTH-GRADERS, A89–A104

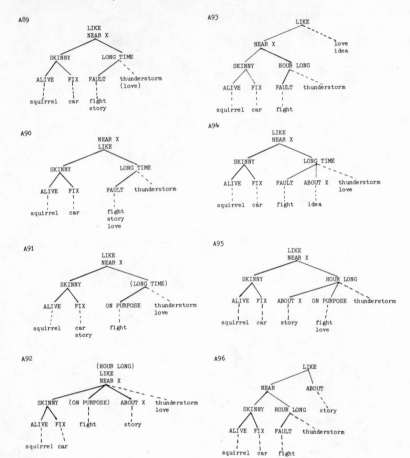

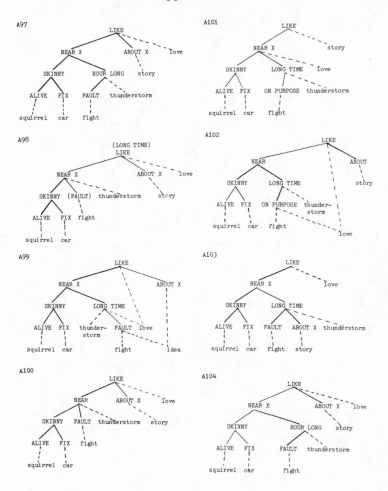

Sixth-Graders, A105–A114

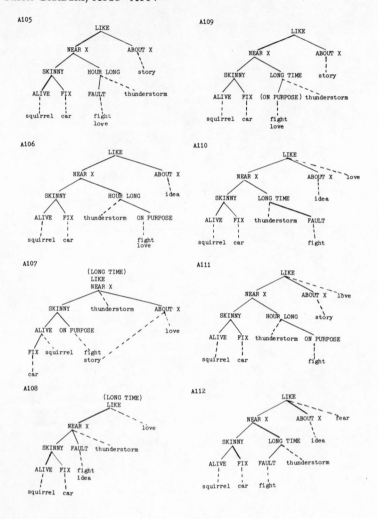

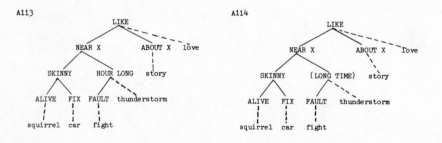

Puerto Rican Study

KINDERGARTNERS, A115–A129

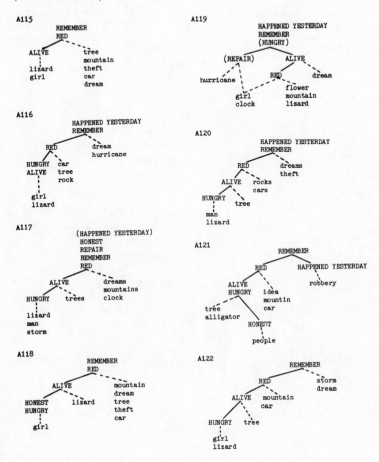

A115

```
        REMEMBER
          RED
ALIVE          tree
               mountain
  lizard       theft
  girl         car
               dream
```

A116

```
            HAPPENED YESTERDAY
            REMEMBER
     RED          dream
                  hurricane
HUNGRY  car
ALIVE   tree
        rock
    girl
    lizard
```

A117

```
              (HAPPENED YESTERDAY)
              HONEST
              REPAIR
              REMEMBER
              RED
   ALIVE          dreams
                  mountains
HUNGRY  trees     clock
  lizard
  man
  storm
```

A118

```
              REMEMBER
                RED
   ALIVE              mountain
                      dream
HONEST  lizard        tree
HUNGRY                theft
  girl                car
```

A119

```
              HAPPENED YESTERDAY
              REMEMBER
              (HUNGRY)
   (REPAIR)         ALIVE
hurricane     RED        dream
              girl   flower
              clock  mountain
                     lizard
```

A120

```
              HAPPENED YESTERDAY
              REMEMBER
        RED          dreams
                     theft
     ALIVE  rocks
            cars
HUNGRY    tree
  man
  lizard
```

A121

```
                    REMEMBER
              RED        HAPPENED YESTERDAY
     ALIVE                    robbery
     HUNGRY   idea
              mountin
tree          car
alligator
        HONEST
          people
```

A122

```
                        REMEMBER
                  RED        storm
                             dream
        ALIVE  mountain
               car
HUNGRY   tree
  girl
  lizard
```

A123

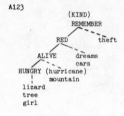

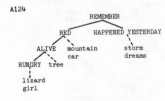

A124

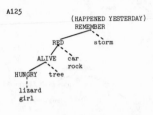

A125

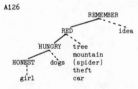

A126

```
                        REMEMBER
                RED  - - - - - idea
           HUNGRY     tree
                      mountain
    HONEST     dogs   (spider)
                      theft
         girl         car
```

A127

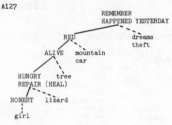

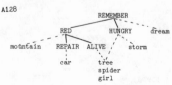

A128

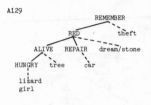

A129

```
                              REMEMBER
                    RED  - - - - - theft
           ALIVE   REPAIR   dream/stone
    HUNGRY   tree      car
       lizard
       girl
```

First-Graders, A130–A144

A130

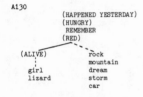

```
                (HAPPENED YESTERDAY)
                (HUNGRY)
                 REMEMBER
                 (RED)

   (ALIVE)         rock
                   mountain
    girl           dream
    lizard         storm
                   car
```

A131

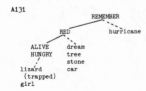

```
                        REMEMBER
            RED                 hurricane

    ALIVE       dream
    HUNGRY      tree
                stone
    lizard      car
    (trapped)
    girl
```

A132

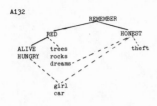

```
                    REMEMBER
       RED                      HONEST
   ALIVE    trees                   theft
   HUNGRY   rocks
            dreams

              girl
              car
```

A133

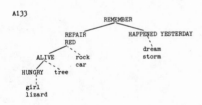

```
                      REMEMBER
         REPAIR               HAPPENED YESTERDAY
         RED
      ALIVE     rock            dream
                car             storm
   HUNGRY   tree
    girl
    lizard
```

A134

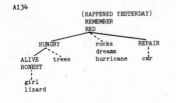

```
                    (HAPPENED YESTERDAY)
                     REMEMBER
                     RED
         HUNGRY        rocks      REPAIR
                       dreams
   ALIVE    trees      hurricane    car
   HONEST
    girl
    lizard
```

A135

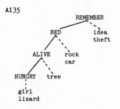

```
                    REMEMBER
         RED            idea
                        theft
     ALIVE    rock
              car
   HUNGRY   tree
    girl
    lizard
```

A136

```
                        REMEMBER
       RED                      HAPPENED YESTERDAY
   ALIVE   REPAIR   tree         dreams
   HUNGRY           rock         theft
              car
   lizard
   girl
```

A137

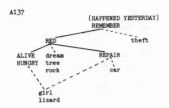

```
                    (HAPPENED YESTERDAY)
                     REMEMBER
         RED                       theft
     ALIVE    dream    REPAIR
     HUNGRY   tree
              rock           car

              girl
              lizard
```

A138

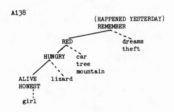

```
                    (HAPPENED YESTERDAY)
                     REMEMBER
         RED            dreams
                        theft
       HUNGRY    car
                 tree
                 mountain
   ALIVE    lizard
   HONEST
    girl
```

A139

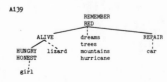

```
                    REMEMBER
                    RED
      ALIVE     dreams           REPAIR
                trees
   HUNGRY  lizard  mountains        car
   HONEST         hurricane
    girl
```

A140

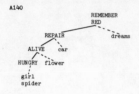

A143

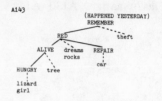

A141

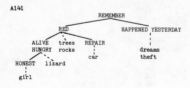

A144

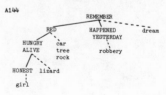

A142

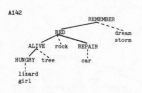

THIRD-GRADERS, A145–A159

A145

A150
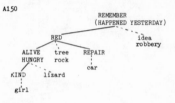

A146
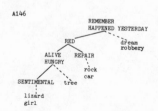

A151
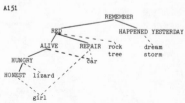

A147
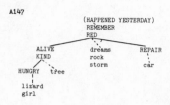

A152
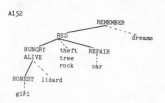

A148
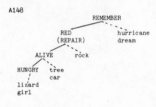

A153
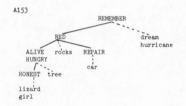

A149
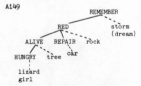

A154
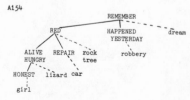

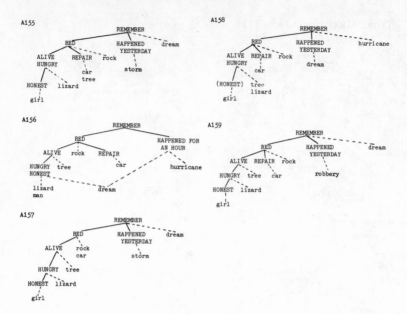

References

ALKER, H. A. A psycholinguistic investigation of a rule theory of "sense." *British Journal of Psychology*, 1966, *57*, 397–403.

ALLWOOD, J., ANDERSSON, L., AND DAHL, O. *Logic in linguistics.* Cambridge: Cambridge University Press, 1977.

ALTHAM, J. E. J. Ambiguity and predication. *Mind*, 1971, *80*, 253–257.

ANGLIN, J. M. The growth of word meaning. Cambridge: M.I.T. Press, 1970.

———. From reference to meaning. Paper presented at biennial meeting of the Society for Research in Child Development, New Orleans, 1975.

———. *Word, object, and conceptual development.* New York: W. W. Norton, 1977.

ARISTOTLE. *Categories,* translated with notes by J. L. Ackrill. London: Oxford University Press, 1963.

ARMSTRONG, S., GLEITMAN, L. R., AND GLEITMAN, H. What most concepts are not, forthcoming.

BERLIN, B., BREEDLOVE, D. E., AND RAVEN, P. H. General principles of classification and nomenclature in folk biology. *American Anthropologist*, 1973, *75*, 214–242.

BERZONSKY, M. The role of familiarity in children's explanations of physical causality. *Child Development*, 1971, *42*, 705–715.

BEVER, T. G., AND LANGENDOEN, D. T. A dynamic model of the evolution of language. *Linguistic Inquiry*, 1971, *2*, 433–463.

BEVER, T. G., AND ROSENBAUM, P. S. Some lexical structures and their empirical validity. In D. D. Steinberg and L. A. Jakobovits (eds.), *Semantics.* Cambridge: Cambridge University Press, 1971.

BILLOW, R. M. Metaphor: A review of the psychological literature. *Psychological Bulletin*, 1977, *85*, 81–92.

BLACK, M. Russell's philosophy of language. In P. A. Schilp (ed.), *The philosophy of Bertrand Russell.* The Library of Living Philosophers, vol. V. Evanston: Northwestern University Press, 1944.

———. Metaphor. *Proceedings of the Aristotelian Society*, 1955, *55*, 271–294.

BLOOM, L. *One word at a time.* The Hague: Mouton, 1973.

BROWN, R. W. *A first language: The early stages.* Cambridge: Harvard University Press, 1973.

BRUNER, J. S., AND BRUNER, B. M. On voluntary action and its hierarchical structure. *International Journal of Psychology,* 1968, *3,* 239–255.

BRUNER, J. S., OLVER, R. R., GREENFIELD, P. M., ET AL. *Studies in cognitive growth.* New York: John Wiley, 1966.

CAREY, S. The child as a word learner. In M. Halle, J. Bresnan, and G. Miller (eds.), *Linguistic theory and psychological reality.* Cambridge: M.I.T. Press, 1978.

———. The child's concepts of animals and living things (tentative title), forthcoming.

CARNAP, R. Empiricism, semantics, and ontology. In R. Carnap (ed.), *Meaning and necessity,* 2nd ed. Chicago: University of Chicago Press, 1956.

CARSTAIRS, A. D. Ryle, Hillman and Harrison on categories. *Mind,* 1971, *80,* 403–408.

CASTENADA, H. Thinking and the structure of the world. *Philosophia,* 1974, *4,* 3–40.

CATON, CHARLES E. Essentially arising questions and the ontology of a natural language. *Nous,* 1971, *5,* 27–38.

CHOMSKY, C. *The acquisition of syntax in children from 5 to 10.* Research Monograph, no. 57. Cambridge: M.I.T. Press, 1969.

CHOMSKY, N. *Aspects of the theory of syntax.* Cambridge: M.I.T. Press, 1965.

———. *Reflections on language.* New York: Pantheon, 1975.

CLARK, E. V. Language acquisition: The child's spontaneous description of events in time. Doctoral dissertation, Department of Linguistics, University of Edinburgh, 1969.

———. On the acquisition of the meaning of "before" and "after." *Journal of Verbal Learning and Verbal Behavior,* 1971, *10,* 266–275.

———. On the child's acquisition of antonyms in two semantic fields. *Journal of Verbal Learning and Verbal Behavior,* 1972, *11,* 750–758.

———. What's in a word? On the child's acquisition of semantics in his first language. In T. E. Moore (ed.), *Cognitive development and the acquisition of language.* New York: Academic Press, 1973.

CLARK, H. H. Space, time, semantics, and the child. In F. E. Moore (ed.), *Cognitive development and the acquisition of language.* New York: Academic Press, 1973.

CLARK, H. H., AND BEGUN, J. S. The semantics of sentence subjects. *Language and Speech,* 1971, *14,* 34–46.

COGAN, R. A criticism of Sommers' language tree. *Notre Dame Journal of Formal Logic,* 1976, *17,* 308–310.

COLLINS, A. M., AND LOFTUS, E. F. A spreading activation theory of semantic processing. *Psychological Review,* 1975, *82,* 407–428.

COLLINS, A. M., AND QUILLIAN, M. R. Retrieval time from semantic memory. *Journal of Verbal Learning and Verbal Behavior,* 1969, *8,* 240–248.

CONRAD, C. E. H. Cognitive economy in semantic memory. *Journal of Experimental Psychology*, 1972, *92*, 149–154.

CORNMAN, J. W. Types, categories, and nonsense. *American Philosophical Quarterly Monographs*, 1968, *2*, 73–97.

———. Categories, grammar and semantics. *Inquiry*, 1970, *13*, 297–307.

CRAMER, P. Evidence for a developmental shift in the basis of memory organization. *Journal of Experimental Child Psychology*, 1973, *16*, 12–22.

———. Idiomatic sets as determinants of children's false recognition errors. *Developmental Psychology*, 1974, *10*, 86–92.

CROSS, R. C. Category differences. *Proceedings of the Aristotelian Society*, 1959, *59*, 264–273.

CULICOVER, P. W., AND WEXLER, K. Some syntactic implications of a theory of language learnability. In P. Culicover, T. Wasow, and A. Akmajian (eds.), *Formal syntax*, pp. 7–60. New York: Academic Press, 1978.

DE SOUSA, R. B. The tree of English bears bitter fruit. *Journal of Philosophy*, 1966, *63*, 37–46.

DEVILLIERS, J. G., AND DEVILLIERS, P. A. Early judgments of syntactic and semantic acceptability. *Journal of Psycholinguistic Research*, 1972, *1*, 299–310.

———. Competence and performance in child language: Are children really competent to judge? *Journal of Child Language*, 1974, *1*, 11–22.

———. *Language acquisition*. Cambridge: Harvard University Press, 1978.

DONALDSON, M., AND WALES, R. J. On the acquisition of some relational terms. In R. J. Hayes (ed.), *Cognition and the development of language*, pp. 235–268. New York: John Wiley and Sons, 1970.

DRANGE, T. *Type crossings*. The Hague: Mouton, 1966.

ELGOOD, A. G. Sommers' rules of sense. *Philosophical Quarterly*, 1970, *20*, 166–169.

ENGLEBRETSEN, G. Sommers' tree theory, possibility, and existence. Doctoral dissertation, University of Nebraska, 1971.

———. On Van Straaten's modification of Sommers' rule. *Philosophical Studies*, 1971a, *23*, 216–219.

———. Persons and predicates. *Philosophical Studies*, 1972, *23*, 393–399.

———. A revised category mistake argument. *Philosophical Studies*, 1972a, *23*, 421–423.

EPSTEIN, W. Recall of word lists following learning of sentences and of anomalous and random strings. *Journal of Verbal Learning and Verbal Behavior*, 1969, *8*, 20–25.

———. Retention of sentences, anomalous sequences and random sequences. *American Journal of Psychology*, 1972, *85*, 21–30.

ERVIN-TRIPP, S. Structure and process in language acquisition. In J. E. Alatais (ed.), *Bilingualism and language contact: Anthropological, psychological, and social aspects*. Monograph Series on Languages and Linguistics, no. 21. Washington, D. C.: Georgetown University Press, 1970.

EWING, A. C. Meaninglessness. *Mind*, 1937, *46*, 347–364.

FJELD, J. Sommers' ontological programme. *Philosophical Studies*, 1974, *25*, 411–416.

FLAVELL, J. Developmental studies of mediated memory. In H. Reese and L. Lipsitt (eds.), *Advances in child development and behavior*, vol. 5. New York: Academic, 1970.

FRANCIS, H. Toward an explanation of the syntactic-paradigmatic shift. *Child Development*, 1972, *43*, 949–958.

FREGE, G. *Foundations of arithmetic*, translated by J. L. Austin. London: Oxford University Press, 1950.

FRIEDMAN, W. J., AND SEELY, P. B. The child's acquisition of spatial and temporal word meanings. *Child Development*, 1976, *47*, 1103–1108.

FRIENDLY, M. L. In search of the M-Gram: The structure of organization in free recall. *Cognitive Psychology*, 1977, *9*, 188–249.

GARDNER, H., KIRCHER, M., WINNER, E., AND PERKINS, D. Children's metaphoric productions and preferences. *Journal of Child Language*, 1975, *2*, 1–17.

GELMAN, R. Cognitive development. *Annual Review of Psychology*, 1978, *29*.

GLASS, A., AND HOLYOAK, K. J. Alternative conceptions of semantic theory. *Cognition*, 1975, *3(4)*, 313–339.

GLEITMAN, H., AND GLEITMAN, L. R. Language use and language judgment. In C. Fillmore and W. Wang, *Individual differences in language ability and language behavior*, Academic Press, in press.

GLEITMAN, L. R., AND GLEITMAN, H. *Phrase and paraphrase*. New York: W. W. Norton, 1970.

GLEITMAN, L. R., GLEITMAN, H., AND SHIPLEY, E. F. The emergence of the child as grammarian. *Cognition*, 1974, *1*, 137–164.

GOODMAN, N. *Fact, fiction, and forecast*. New York: Bobbs Merrill, 1965.

GREENFIELD, P. M., AND SCHNEIDER, L. Building a tree structure: The development of hierarchical complexity and interrupted strategies in children's construction activity. *Developmental Psychology*, 1977, *13*, 299–313.

GUERRY, H. Sommers' ontological proof. *Analysis*, 1967, *27*, 60–61.

HAACK, S. Equivocality: A discussion of Sommers' views. *Analysis*, 1968, *28*, 159–165.

HARRIS, P. L. Inferences and semantic development. *Journal of Child Language*, 1975, *2*, 143–152.

HARRISON, B. Category mistakes and rules of language. *Mind*, 1965, *74*, 309–325.

HAVILAND, S. E., AND CLARK, E. V. "This man's father is my father's son": A study of the acquisition of English kin terms. *Journal of Child Language*, 1974, *1*, 23–47.

HEIDENHEIMER, P. A comparison of the roles of exemplar, action, coordinate, and superordinate relations in the semantic processing of 4- and 5-year-old children. *Journal of Experimental Child Psychology*, 1978, 25, 143–159.

HILLMAN, D. J. On grammars and category mistakes. *Mind*, 1963, 72, 224–234.

HOWE, H. E., AND HILLMAN, D. J. The acquisition of semantic restrictions in children. *Journal of Verbal Learning and Verbal Behavior*, 1973, 12, 132–139.

HUANG, I. Children's conception of physical causality: A critical summary. *Journal of Genetic Psychology*, 1943, 63, 71–121.

HUGHES, G. E., AND CRESSWELL, M. J. *An introduction to modal logic*. London: Methuen, 1968.

INHELDER, B., AND PIAGET, J. *The early growth of logic in the child*. New York: W. W. Norton, 1964.

JACKENDOFF, R. *Semantic interpretation in generative grammar*. Cambridge: M.I.T. Press, 1972.

———. Toward an explanatory semantic representation. *Linguistic Inquiry*, 1976, 7, 89–150.

JAMES, S. L., AND MILLER, J. F. Children's awareness of semantic constraints in sentences. *Child Development*, 1973, 44, 69–75.

KATZ, J. J. *The philosophy of language*. New York: Harper and Row, 1966.

———. *Semantic theory*. New York: Harper and Row, 1972.

KATZ, J. J., AND FODOR, J. A. The structure of a semantic theory. *Language*, 1963, 39, 190–210.

KEENAN, E. Logical semantics and universal grammar. *Theoretical Linguistics*, in press.

KEIL, F. C. The development of the ability to perceive ambiguities: Evidence for the task specificity of a linguistic skill. *Journal of Psycholinguistic Research*, in press.

KLINGBERG, G. The distinction between living and non-living among 7–10-year-old children, with some remarks concerning the animism controversy. *Journal of Genetic Psychology*, 1957, 90, 227–238.

KOSLOWSKI, B. Acquiring the concept of causation. Manuscript, 1978.

KRIPKE, S. Naming and necessity. In D. Davidson and G. Harmon (eds.), *Semantics of natural language*. Boston: D. Reidel, 1972.

———. Oral presentation at Cornell University, 1978.

LAURENDEAU, M., AND PINARD, A. *Causal thinking in the child: A genetic and experimental approach*. New York: International Universities Press, 1962.

LEECH, G. *Semantics*. Middlesex, Eng.: Penguin Books, 1974.

LOFTUS, E. F. How to catch a zebra in semantic memory. In R. Shaw and J. Bransford (eds.), *Perceiving, acting and knowing: Toward an ecological psychology*. Hillsdale, N. J.: Lawrence Erlbaum Associates, 1977.

LOOFT, W. R., AND BARTZ, W. H. Animism revised. *Psychological Bulletin*, 1969, 71, 1–19.

McCawley, J. D. The role of semantics in a grammar. In E. Bach and R. T. Harms (eds.), *Universals in linguistic theory.* New York: Holt, 1968.

Mansfield, A. F. Semantic organization in the young child: Evidence for the development of semantic feature systems. *Journal of Experimental Child Psychology*, 1977, *23*, 57–77.

Margand, N. A. Perceptual and semantic features in children's use of the animate concept. *Developmental Psychology*, 1977, *13*, 572–576.

Markman, E. M. Children's difficulty with word-referent differentiation. *Child Development*, 1976, *47*, 742–749.

Markman, E. M., and Siebert, J. Classes and collections: Internal organization and resulting holistic properties. *Cognitive Psychology*, 1976, *8*, 561–577.

Marks, L. E., and Miller, G. A. The role of semantic and syntactic constraints in the memorization of English sentences. *Journal of Verbal Learning and Verbal Behavior*, 1964, *3*, 1–5.

Marshall, J. C. A note on semantic theory. In G. B. Flores-D'Arcais and W. J. M. Levelt (eds.), *Advances in Psycholinguistics.* Amsterdam: North Holland Publishing, 1970.

Martin, J. A many-valued semantics for category mistakes. *Synthese*, 1975, *31*, 63–83.

Massie, D. Sommers' tree theory: A reply to DeSousa. *Journal of Philosophy*, 1967, *64*, 185–193.

Meyer, D. E. On the representation and retrieval of stored semantic information. *Cognitive Psychology*, 1970, *1*, 242–299.

Miller, G. A., and Isard, S. Some perceptual consequences of linguistic rules. *Journal of Verbal Learning and Verbal Behavior*, 1963, *2*, 217–228.

Nelson, J. O. On Sommers' restatement of Russell's ontological programme. *Philosophical Review*, 1964, *73*, 517–521.

Nelson, K. The syntagmatic-paradigmatic shift revisited: A review of research and theory. *Psychological Bulletin*, 1977, *84*, 93–116.

Osherson, D. N. *Logical abilities in children.* New York: John Wiley, 1976.

———. Natural connectives: A Chomskyan approach. *Journal of Mathematical Psychology*, 1977, *16*, 1–29.

———. Three conditions on conceptual naturalness. *Cognition*, 1978, *6*, 263–289.

Osherson, D. N., and Markman, E. Language and the ability to evaluate contradictions and tautologies. *Cognition*, 1974, *3*, 213–226.

Osherson, D. N., and Wasow, T. Task-specificity and species-specificity in the study of language: A methodological note. *Cognition*, 1976, *4*, 203–214.

Palermo, D. S. More about less: A study of language comprehension. *Journal of Verbal Learning and Verbal Behavior*, 1973, *12*, 211–221.

Pap, A. Types and meaninglessness. *Mind*, 1960, *69*, 41–54.

Parsons, J. E., Ruble, D. N., Klosson, E. C., Feldman, N. S., and

RHOLES, W. S. Order effects on children's moral and achievement judgments. *Developmental Psychology,* 1976, *12,* 357–358.

PASSELL, D. On Sommers' logic of sense and nonsense. *Mind,* 1969, *78,* 132–133.

PIAGET, J. *The child's conception of the world.* New York: Harcourt, Brace, 1929.

———. *The child's conception of physical causality.* New York: Harcourt, Brace, 1930.

———. *The moral judgment of the child.* New York: Free Press, 1965 (originally published, 1932).

POLLIO, H. R., AND BURNS, B. C. The anomaly of anomaly. *Journal of Psycholinguistic Research,* 1977, *6,* 247–260.

PRIOR, A. N. The meaning of logical connectives. *Analysis,* 1967, *21,* 38–39.

PUTNAM, J. The meaning of meaning. In H. Putnam (ed.), *Mind, language, and reality,* vol. 2. London: Cambridge University Press, 1975.

QUINE, W. V. O. Two dogmas of empiricism. In W. V. O. Quine (ed.), *From a logical point of view.* Cambridge: Harvard University Press, 1953.

———. *Word and object,* Cambridge: M.I.T. Press, 1960.

RIEGEL, K. F. Relational interpretation of the language acquisition process. In G. B. Flores-D'Arcais and W. J. M. Levelt (eds.), *Advances in Psycholinguistics.* Amsterdam: North Holland Publishing, 1970.

ROSCH, E. On the internal structure of perceptual and semantic categories. In T. E. Moore (ed.), *Cognitive development and the acquisition of language.* New York: Academic Press, 1973.

———. Universals and cultural specifics in human categorization. In R. Breslin, W. Lonner, and S. Bochner (eds.), *Cross-cultural perspectives in learning.* London: Sage Press, 1974.

ROSCH, E., AND MERVIS, C. Family resemblances: Studies in the internal structure of categories. *Cognitive Psychology,* 1975, *7,* 573–605.

ROSCH, E., MERVIS, C. B., GRAY, W. D., JOHNSON, D., AND BOYES-BRAEM, P. Basic objects in natural categories. *Cognitive Psychology,* 1976, *8,* 382–439.

RUSSELL, B. Logical atomism. In J. H. Muirhead (ed.), *Contemporary British philosophy,* 1st series. London: G. Allen and Unwin, 1924.

RUSSELL, R. W. Studies in animism: The development of animism. *Journal of Genetic Psychology,* 1940, *56,* 353–366.

RYLE, G. Categories. *Proceedings of the Aristotelian Society,* 1938, *38,* 189–206.

SAVIN, H. Meanings and concepts: A review of Jerrold J. Katz's semantic theory. *Cognition,* 1973, *2,* 213–238.

SAYWARD, C. A defense of Sommers. *Philosophical Studies,* 1976, *29,* 343–347.

SAYWARD, C., AND VOSS, S. H. Absurdity and spanning. *Philosophia,* 1972, *2,* 227–238.

SIMON, H. A. *The sciences of the artificial.* Cambridge: M.I.T. Press, 1969.

SINCLAIR, H. Sensori-motor action patterns as the condition for the acquisition of syntax. In R. Huxley and E. Ingrams (eds.), *Language acquisition: Models and methods.* New York: Academic Press, 1971.

SMART, J. J. C. A note on categories. *The British Journal of the Philosophy of Science,* 1953, *5,* 227–228.

SMITH, E. E. Theories of semantic memory. In W. K. Estes (ed.), *Handbook of learning and cognitive processes,* vol. 6: *Linguistic functions in cognitive theory.* Hillsdale, N. J. Lawrence Erlbaum Associates, 1978.

SMITH, E. E., SHOBEN, E. J., AND RIPS, L. J. Structure and process in semantic memory: A featural model for semantic decisions. *Psychological Review,* 1974, *81,* 214–241.

SOMMERS, F. The ordinary language tree. *Mind,* 1959, *68,* 160–185.

———. Types and ontology. *Philosophical Review,* 1963, *72,* 327–363.

———. Meaning relations and the analytic. *Journal of Philosophy,* 1963a, *60,* 524–534.

———. A program for coherence. *Philosophical Review,* 1964, *73,* 522 527.

———. Predicability. In M. Black (ed.), *Philosophy in America.* Ithaca: Cornell University Press, 1965.

———. Do we need identity? *Journal of Philosophy,* 1969, *66,* 499–504.

———. The calculus of terms. *Mind,* 1970, *79,* 1–39.

———. Structural ontology. *Philosophia,* 1971, *1,* 21–42.

———. On predication and logical syntax. In A. Kasher (ed.), *Language in focus: Formulations, methods, and systems.* Boston: D. Reidel, 1976.

STEINBERG, D. D. Analyticity, amphigory, and semantic interpretation of sentences. *Journal of Verbal Learning and Verbal Behavior,* 1970, *9,* 37–51.

———. Negation, analyticity, amphigory, and the semantic interpretation of sentences. *Journal of Experimental Psychology,* 1970a, *84,* 417–423.

———. Truth, amphigory, and the semantic interpretation of sentences. *Journal of Experimental Psychology,* 1972, *93,* 217–218.

STEINBERG, E. R., AND ANDERSON, R. C. Hierarchical semantic organization in 6 year olds. *Journal of Experimental Child Psychology,* 1975, *19,* 544–553.

STEVENSON, L. On what sorts of things there are. *Mind,* 1976, *85,* 503–521.

STRAWSON, P. F. Categories. In O. P. Wood and G. Pitcher (eds.), *Ryle: A collection of critical essays.* Garden City, N. Y.: Doubleday, 1970.

TOWNSEND, D. J., AND ERB, M. Children's strategies for interpreting complex comparative questions. *Journal of Child Language,* 1975, *2,* 271–277.

TVERSKY, A. Features of Similarity. *Psychological Review*, 1977, *84*, 327–352.

VAN STRAATEN, R. A modification of Sommers' rule. *Philosophical Studies*, 1971, *22*, 16–20.

VYGOTSKY, L. S. *Thought and language*. Cambridge: M.I.T. Press, 1965.

WALL, R. *Introduction to mathematical linguistics*. Englewood Cliffs, N.J.: Prentice-Hall, 1972.

WERNER, H. *Comparative psychology of mental development*. New York: Harper and Brothers, 1940.

WERNER, H., AND KAPLAN, B. *Symbol formation*. New York: John Wiley and Sons, 1963.

WEXLER, K. Empirical questions about developmental psycholinguistics raised by a theory of language acquisition. In R. N. Campbell and P. T. Smith (eds.), *Recent advances in the psychology of language*. New York: Plenum Publishing, 1978.

WOODS, J. Semantic kinds. *Philosophia*, 1973, *3*, 117–152.

Author Index

Subject Index

adequacy: of syntactic theory, 7
ff.; observational, 7–8; descriptive, 8; explanatory, 8,
17, 63, 171
ambiguity, 12, 29, 66; and M
constraint, 16
animism, 131 ff.
anomaly, 3, 18, 26 ff., 54 ff., 65,
119
antonymous *n*-tuples, 66
artifacts, functional, 85, 116
associative relatedness, 49

"beads-on-a-string" model, 75,
103

categories: ontological, 7, 11 ff.,
48, 156, 161; basic level, 50;
natural, 50 ff.; superordinate,
50 ff.; developing out of
others, 78, 105
category mistakes, 16, 54–55,
140 ff.
causality, 130
classes: natural and non-natural,
4, 19; without unique predicates, 153
classification, 133 ff.
collapses, of adjacent categories,
76, 102 ff., 114–116
conceivability, 143 ff., 156, 163
concepts, natural, 5, 161 ff., 171

configurational changes, tree
structure, 87
constraints, 1, 63 ff., 163, 165 ff.
contextual influences on meaning, 151
contradictions, copredictations
involving, 5, 144 ff.
copredications, natural and non-
natural, 4, 21
criterial attributes, 50 ff.

de dicto modality, 155
de re modality, 156
definitional vs. presuppositional
features, 52, 145 ff.
developmental research, 119
differentiae, 11–12
differentiation: of predicability
trees, 74, 102, 113; asymmetric, 75, 79, 103–104, 113; ordered, 75, 103–104, 113
dominance, of nodes, 19
downward tree proliferation,
140–147

ellipsis, 4, 55, 153
empirical laws, possible and
impossible, 6, 130, 154 ff.
empirical plausibility, 81 ff.
entailment, 5
essentially arising questions,
157

212